Mending a Tattered Faith

art for faith's sake series

SERIES EDITORS:

Clayton J. Schmit
J. Frederick Davison

This series of publications is designed to promote the creation of resources for the church at worship. It promotes the creation of two types of material, what we are calling primary and secondary liturgical art.

Like primary liturgical theology, classically understood as the actual prayer and practice of people at worship, primary liturgical art is that which is produced to give voice to God's people in public prayer or private devotion and art that is created as the expression of prayerful people. Secondary art, like secondary theology, is written reflection on material that is created for the sake of the prayer, praise, and meditation of God's people.

The series presents both worship art and theological and pedagogical reflection on the arts of worship. The series title, *Art for Faith's Sake*,* indicates that, while some art may be created for its own sake, a higher purpose exists for arts that are created for use in prayer and praise.

TITLES IN THIS SERIES:

Praying the Hours in Ordinary Life by Lauralee Farrer
     and Clayton J. Schmit
Preaching Master Class by William H. Willimon
Dust and Ashes by James L. Crenshaw
Dust and Prayers by Charles L. Bartow
Senses of the Soul by William A. Dyrness

FORTHCOMING TITLES:

Teaching Hymnal by Clayton J. Schmit

* *Art for Faith's Sake* is a phrase coined by art collector and church musician, Jerry Evenrud, to whom we are indebted.

Mending a Tattered Faith

Devotions with Dickinson

Susan VanZanten

CASCADE *Books* · Eugene, Oregon

MENDING A TATTERED FAITH
Devotions with Dickinson

Art for Faith's Sake 6

Cascade Books
An Imprint of Wipf and Stock Publishers
199 W. 8th Ave., Suite 3
Eugene, OR 97401
www.wipfandstock.com

ISBN 13: 978-1-60899-510-3

Cataloging-in-Publication data:

VanZanten, Susan.

    Mending a tattered faith : devotions with Dickinson / Susan VanZanten.

    xxxii + 86 p. ; 23 cm. —Includes bibliographical references.

    Art for Faith's Sake 6

    ISBN 13: 978-1-60899-510-3

    1. Dickinson, Emily, 1830–1886. Correspondence. 2. Dickinson, Emily, 1830–1886. Poems. 3. Dickinson, Emily, 1830–1886—Religion. I. Title. II. Series.

PS1541.Z5 V25 2011

With gratitude to Marti and Anna—

—imperceptible yet strong pillars—

Contents

Acknowledgments

My imperceptible pillars join a host of more visible supporters who have helped me through both this book and the last three years of my life. Above all, I thank my family: Shirley and Paul VanZanten, Joseph VanZanten Gallagher, Sandi and Keith Guard, Barbara and Michael Burkhalter, and Scott VandeKieft. Other rocks include Cindy Price, Debbie and Jim Crouch, Les Steele, Chris Chaney, Denise Daniels, Bob Drovdahl, Joyce Erickson, Fan Gates, and Nancy Lucas Williams.

Introduction, or, How to Read This Book

Mending a Tattered Faith is a collection of meditative explorations intended to help you both to enjoy Emily Dickinson's poetry and to think about spiritual issues. It is neither a traditional biography of Dickinson nor a scholarly interpretation of her work. Rather, it attempts to facilitate and encourage reflection. "Devotions" may be a misleading term if you think that devotions necessarily conclude with a homily, a message, or a clear answer. Dickinson was oddly both a Queen of ambiguous complexity and an Empress of vivid detail; her poems raise pointed questions and consider possible responses but seldom result in Definite Answers. But such open-endedness can lead to pondering.

Mary, the mother of Christ, was one who pondered. When the angel Gabriel showed up on her doorstep and declared that she was highly favored of God, Mary was "much perplexed by his words and pondered what sort of greeting this might be" (Luke 1:29, NRSV). Again, when her child was born during an unexpected journey to Bethlehem and rough shepherds arrived at the stable with an outlandish story about angels, Mary "treasured all these things and pondered them in her heart" (Luke 2:19, NRSV). Twelve years later, Mary is still pondering when Jesus disappears during a trip to Jerusalem and turns up three days later talking with the temple scholars. Once again the NRSV uses the verb "treasured" to speak of the way that Mary saves, thinks about, and prizes these events (Luke 2:51). Mary engages in ongoing reflection in response to these events, despite her many unanswered questions. It is such mental weighing, such probing of possibilities that Dickinson's poems prompt.

Although there are several good biographical accounts of Dickinson's personal struggles with faith, I don't think we will ever be able to grasp fully all the nuances of her pilgrim life. Dickinson's letters provide glimpses of different spiritual states at different points in her life, but because so many of them are missing—either destroyed by her family when she died or yet to be located—such glimpses provide only isolated snapshots of her spiritual journey. The poems provide even less reliable evidence. While there are physical difficulties in dating many of them and deciphering Dickinson's handwriting, a greater problem lies in the fact that we can never be sure whether the voice speaking in a poem represents the personal feelings of the poet or is an assumed mask or *persona* used to create a poetic effect. Dickinson herself claimed that the speaker of her poems was not herself but a "supposed person" (Letter 268). When that voice speaks to us from the grave or refers to itself as a boy—both of which occur in several poems—it is obvious that some degree of fictionalizing is taking place. Similarly, when a poem professes deep faith, mocks Christian assurance, reverently addresses a watchful God, or derisively attacks a cruel deity, should we see it as representing Dickinson's own beliefs or dramatically depicting a particular position? It is true that Dickinson often sent poems to her friends, almost as if a poem was a letter, or an addendum to a letter. But *if* we do assume a high degree of identification between the poetic voice and Dickinson, what do we make of the fact that the poems as a whole neither consistently affirm either faith or doubt, nor clearly trace a chronological progress from one state to another?

It doesn't disturb me, though, that her poems cannot answer ultimate questions about Dickinson's spiritual state. While as a literary scholar I could argue for a particular interpretation of each poem, based upon textual evidence as well as historical, cultural, social, and—yes—biographical context, in this book, I am not going to present such arguments. Rather, I'd like to encourage you to sit with a Dickinson poem for a while in silence, reflecting on the images and issues it raises, the memories or experiences it prompts, and the glimpses of truth that it unveils.

Like all well-bred nineteenth-century New England women, Emily Dickinson knew how to wield a needle, although she much preferred working in her garden or roaming the woods in search of wildflowers. She used her sewing ability in one unusual fashion: sometime in 1858, when she was twenty-seven years old, she began to construct small books of her poetry. She started by neatly copying selected poems in ink onto sheets of heavy stationary that she then sewed together into a small booklet with a needle and thread, punching two holes near the fold on the left-hand side and tying the thread in the front. Scholars call these little self-published books *fascicles*, which means a small bunch or bundle of something. In botany, a fascicle refers to a cluster of plant parts, such as branches, leaves, or stems, which is especially appropriate as Dickinson also often referred to her poems as flowers.

Most nineteenth-century women, however, would use their needles for mending clothes and stockings, and it is this ability to repair something that is "tattered" or frayed that Dickinson refers to in a poem written late in her life:

> To mend each tattered Faith
> There is a needle fair
> Though no appearance indicate –
> 'Tis threaded in the Air –
>
> And though it do not wear
> As if it never Tore
> 'Tis very comfortable indeed
> And spacious as before –[1]

The poem presents a metaphorical picture of faith as a torn article of clothing that needs mending—a scriptural image to the extent that the Bible often refers to salvation using the metaphor of clothing, as in Isaiah's "garments of salvation" and "robe of righteousness" (61:10),[2] or the wedding garment Jesus talks about in the parable in Matthew 22. But in the poem we find faith that has been "tattered" by some kind of experience or perhaps doubt. In the poem's description, the mending tool—the needle—is both beautiful as well as reasonable (implied by the pun on the word *fair*), despite the paradox that it cannot be seen and is "threaded in the Air." Could this invisible needle and thread be referring to the work of the Holy Spirit, the unseen presence that sustains the Christian in times of difficulty and doubt? We often think of the Holy Spirit as associated with air, with the mighty rushing wind that filled the house where the apostles were gathered on the day of Pentecost. The poem's later mention of "comfort" also evokes language associated with the third member of the Trinity.

---

1. Poem 1442 in *The Poems of Emily Dickinson*, edited by Thomas H. Johnson.

2. Unless otherwise noted, all biblical quotations come from the Authorized King James Version, the version read by Dickinson and her family.

After affirming ("there is") this mysterious and beautiful seamstress, the poem's second stanza describes the results of the repair job. The garment of Faith has not been restored exactly to its previous condition; something is different; perhaps a patch can be seen; perhaps the wearer can't move in a certain way. But, nonetheless, the garment is still "comfortable" and "spacious," thanks to the ministrations of the invisible seamstress. When we have doubts that are overcome, our faith is changed, and we will never return to our earlier simpler affirmations. Yet a repaired faith can bring comfort or relief from anxiety, as well as more mental room, a larger thought-world in which to dwell. Perhaps Dickinson's poems can similarly help us repair our own tattered garments of faith.

This book attempts to help you think about Dickinson's poems by using some common interpretive tools, because I think this guidance is one way (among others) to facilitate spiritual mending. While these meditations will refer to and occasionally explain the poems' literary devices, as well as provide some historical and biographical background, this information is not given in order to claim, "This is what this poem definitively means." Rather, I give this information in order to suggest, "These are ways in which this poem might prompt us to think." Jeanne Murray Walker, a contemporary Christian poet, reminds us, "A poem is meant to be an experience, not propositional truth,"[3] and this series of meditations is intended to help you enter into such an experience. I hope that reading and thinking about Dickinson's poems may provide you with a way of listening for God or naming your own spiritual doubts and fears. May her literary gifts facilitate both mending and treasuring.

Here are a few suggestions for ways to use this book, although you certainly should feel free to employ whatever strategies are personally most effective. I would not advise tackling more than one poem at a single sitting. Start by reading the poem aloud once and then silently a second time. Then sit and think about it for a while and perhaps even explore in writing what you think it means, the questions it raises, and the ways in which it speaks to you. A brief prompt for such mental or written reflection is included after each poem, if you wish to use it. Then read and work through the commentary that follows each poem. I suspect that you'll find that you need to go back and forth between the poem and the commentary. Finally, return to the poem itself for a final ponder.

3. Walker, "A Comment," 100.

A Poet's Sewing Kit

Despite the brevity of Dickinson's poems, many people find them difficult to read. Some of that difficulty comes from her idiosyncratic poetic techniques, such as her use of dashes for punctuation, sporadic capitalization, fractured syntax, and unusual rhyme and meter. We may be tempted to assume that Dickinson simply didn't know what she was doing, but from her manuscripts and letters we know that she deliberately chose her atypical techniques, labored over poems to craft their form, and experimented with different versions or alternative word choices. Her extensive reading in contemporary poetry and resistance to her friends' efforts to edit her work indicate that she knew what nineteenth-century poetry was supposed to look like; she just didn't want to write that way.

Dickinson's poems have been compared to supercharged batteries or ever-growing snowballs that acquire more layers as they roll along, but I have thought of them as Instant Animals ever since my son was two years old, and we were devising strategies to keep him entertained during meals at restaurants. Instant Animals come out of the diaper bag looking like a cold capsule (parents need to be careful that young children don't swallow them!). You drop the pill into a glass of water, and watch in amazement (or at least a two-year-old does) as the capsule gradually dissolves and the internal matter slowly grows into, *voila*, a pink elephant, or an orange giraffe, or a purple lion. Then, you can take the Instant Animal out of the water glass and parade it around the bread plates and water glasses. How one small capsule can unfold into such a delightful toy may appear magical but actually depends on the capability of a sponge to absorb liquid and expand far beyond its dehydrated state.

Dickinson's poems are similarly distilled. They achieve a single moment of intensity, of thought condensed to its essence, like oranges pressed into juice that is further squeezed into concentrate. In one of her poems, Dickinson described the poet almost as such a kitchen implement "That / Distills amazing sense / From Ordinary Meanings." A poet, she continues, produces "Attar so immense / From the familiar species / That perished by the Door," that we are surprised we had not previously noticed the strong scent.[4] Such "immense" effects are created through assiduous use of a number of poetic techniques. If we pay attention to these

4. Poem 446 in *The Poems: Variorum*, edited by Ralph W. Franklin. Unless otherwise indicated, all poems are from this edition.

strategies as we read the poems, we provoke more of their meanings to emerge, more of the cells of the sponge to expand and reveal a shape or form, idea or emotion.

Having a basic grasp of some of Dickinson's most common poetic tools thus will better equip us to read and unpack the poems. Perhaps the most important tool, the primary needle in her sewing kit, is diction, or word choice. Emily Dickinson loved words and paid painstaking attention to them. She delighted in the way they sounded, their minute differences of denotation, the rich resources of their connotations. After she began to write poetry seriously in her late twenties, she wrote a friend, "We used to think, Joseph, when I was an unsifted girl and you so scholarly that words were cheap & weak. Now I dont [sic] know of anything so mighty. There are [those] to which I lift my hat when I see them sitting princelike among their peers on the page. Sometimes I write one, and look at his outlines till he glows as no sapphire."[5] Dickinson's hand-written manuscripts reveal her experimenting with words, trying out a variety of choices for a single line. Even in the final "fair" copies of the fascicles, she frequently included alternative readings, putting a mark before a word and then noting an alternative word after the mark in the side or lower margin of the page. For example, Poem 833 begins

> Pain – expands the Time-
> Ages +coil within
> The minute Circumference
> Of a single Brain –

At the bottom of Dickinson's handwritten page, "+lurk" is given as an alternative for "coil." Each word has a slightly different connotation, a faintly different emotional feel. Her inclusion of such alternatives contributes to her poetry's unusually high degree of open-endedness and encouragement of multiple readings.

One of Dickinson's most indispensable tools was her "Lexicon," or dictionary, which her niece described her as reading "as a priest [reads] his breviary—over and over, page by page."[6] Dickinson regularly consulted Noah Webster's *American Dictionary of the English Language* (probably the 1844 edition) while writing her poems, drawing on Webster's

---

5. Sewell, *The Lyman Letters*, 78.

6. Bianchi, *Life and Letters*, 80.

definitions as well as etymologies. The great American lexicographer had spoken when the cornerstone of the local Amherst College was laid, and his granddaughter was one of Emily's childhood friends. So when we read Dickinson's rich poems, we do well to keep our own dictionaries close at hand in order to explore a word's multiple denotations and to "lift our hat" when a particularly splendid word-prince passes by. Dickinson had a special delight in puns, which are so slyly inserted in many poems that they may escape our first or even second reading, as in the way she uses *fair* in "To mend each tattered Faith." Similarly, when she speaks of the poet as the one who "distills amazing sense / From Ordinary Meanings," *sense* is a pun for *scents*, in the perfume metaphor created with subsequent references to attar and flowers.

The high esteem that Dickinson felt for words frequently inspired her to grant some of them the further distinction of capitalization. We know that she studied German at school, a language in which all nouns are capitalized, but we can't identify a clear pattern in her usage, and the appearance of a capital often seems whimsical or capricious. In addition, since her handwriting is exceedingly difficult to read, whether a word is capitalized or not is sometimes unclear. Often, though, we can identify a pattern of linkage: with an Image and an Idea resonating through the visual connection provided by capitalization. We will be on the lookout for these.

Dickinson's dashes are even more puzzling, although it is helpful to know that during her time it was considered stylish to use dashes when writing letters. Both her sister and her brother used them in their correspondence. Perhaps they are another indication that Dickinson's poems are "my letter[s] to the World," as Poem 519 puts it. The dashes produce a rhythm, add emphases, generate spaces of silence, and—most noticeably—create deliberate ambiguity in grammar and syntax. Should we read dashes as periods, colons, or commas? Do they indicate some vague length of a pause somewhere between a period and a comma? Take a line like "My Basket holds – just – Firmaments" (Poem 358). The dashes add more ambiguity to the already uncertain grammar. Is *just* functioning as an adverb (as in "only") or as an adjective (as in "fair, right, impartial")? Or does it simultaneously mean both by prompting us to ask about the meaning of both? Such poetic disjunction—unclear parts of speech—is common in Dickinson's poetry.

Even the most familiar elements of poetry, rhyme and meter, take unusual contours in Dickinson's work. Although she does draw on what we most commonly think of as rhyme—perfect rhyme at the end of lines (*saw/raw*)—she also often holds lines together more tentatively with imperfect rhyme (*abroad/head; crumb/home*). But Dickinson's favorite kinds of rhymes are those that appear within rather than at the end of a poetic line: alliteration, assonance, and consonance. In alliteration, an initial consonant or vowel sound is repeated: "*O*ars divide the *O*cean" or "*B*rave *B*obolink." In assonance, vowel sounds within words are repeated: "And r*o*wed him s*o*fter H*o*me." And in consonance, the final consonants in stressed syllables agree (u*p*/ste*p*; whi*le*/hi*ll*). These are subtle ways in which to create certain sounds and emotional effects and also to hint at connecting ideas, as we will see.

Dickinson's "spasmodic" gait, or fluctuating meter, particularly annoyed some of her nineteenth-century readers although readers today tend not to be as annoyed by such shifts.[7] She rarely uses the gold standard of metrical poetry, the weighty iambic pentameter of Shakespeare or Milton, preferring instead to write most often in common meter—the meter that is sometimes called "sixes and sevens" and is frequently employed in traditional hymnody. The church that Dickinson attended for almost thirty years had the popular *Psalms, Hymns, and Spiritual Songs, of the Rev. Isaac Watts, D.D. to Which Are Added Select Hymns, from Other Authors* for its hymnal, and many of its songs are in common meter.

In several of her letters, Dickinson refers to her poems as hymns or psalms. Common meter has a stanza of four lines (a quatrain), with the first and third lines having eight syllables with four strong stresses, and the second and fourth having six syllables with three strong stresses. Common meter also follows an iambic pattern, in which an unaccented (˘) syllable is followed by an accented (/) syllable. For example,

> There is a fountain filled with blood
> Drawn from Emmanuel's veins
> And sinners plunged beneath that flood
> Lose all their guilty stains.

Congregations need this kind of regular rhythm in order to sing together, but Dickinson's poetic songs range more freely at times by adding an ex-

---

7. See Letter 265.

tra syllable, dropping a strong stress, or inserting a trochee, in which an accented syllable is followed by an unaccented one, as in the word *angels*. Once again subtle effects of feeling and meaning are formed through delicate employment of sound. You can probably already see how important it is to read Dickinson's poems out loud in order to fully savor them.

If diction is the needle in Dickinson's sewing kit, metaphor is her thread. All poets, including William Cooper (who wrote "There Is a Fountain Filled with Blood"), work extensively with metaphor, a figure of speech involving the identification of one object with another in order to ascribe to the first object some of the qualities of the second. In metaphors, we take a word or words from one context and apply it to a new context. In Poem 446, Dickinson takes words from the context of making perfume and applies them to the new context of writing poetry. This allows us imaginatively to consider the ways in which a poem is like perfume: sweet, beautiful, concentrated, derived from nature, a work of effort, etc. Metaphors have both referential and emotive characteristics; they are highly allusive rather than precise. They may be simple, prompting a single comparison, or complex, when a series of interconnected metaphors are used to structure an entire poem (often called a *controlling metaphor*), as in the basic metaphor of faith as a garment, which gives rise to *tattered, needle, threaded, wear, tore, comfortable*. As we read Dickinson's poetry, we will spend a good deal of time unpacking the metaphors, for metaphor, as Roger Lundin explains, "serves as the primary means by which we make intellectual discoveries. Through metaphors, we can see similarities and possibilities we never before imagined."[8]

All of these poetic techniques—diction, capitalization, punctuation, rhyme, meter, and metaphor—provide the means by which Dickinson compresses intense and fertile meaning into relatively brief poems. Each technique functions like one more pebble dropped in the pond of meaning, creating new ripples and waves, some of which overlap, some of which contend against each other, but all of which paint a complex picture.

Emily Dickinson's Life

Depending on which poems and biographies we read, we find many different Emily Dickinsons. As one of her early biographers says, "She is

---

8. Gallagher and Lundin, *Literature through the Eyes of Faith*, 26.

inexhaustible."[9] There is Dickinson the nature poet and Dickinson the love poet; the depressed Dickinson, the oppressed Dickinson, the rebellious Dickinson; there is Dickinson the romantic, the feminist, or the modernist. And then there is the Dickinson who wrote profound poems about faith and doubt—some of which affirm the side of faith; others of which dwell in doubt.

It's tempting, when teaching Dickinson's poetry, to try to construct a consistent or coherent picture. Many of my college students tell me that in high school they were introduced to the poet of doubt, the poet who sardonically terms Faith "a fine invention," who rebelliously revels in observing the Sabbath in her garden rather than by attending church, and who audaciously calls God "a mastiff." Dickinson's first editors, Thomas Wentworth Higginson and Mabel Loomis Todd, leaned in the opposite direction, softening Dickinson's apparent religious infidelity in their editing of the first edition of her poetry that was published four years after her death. For example, in a poem called "I asked no other thing," these overly zealous editors changed God's *sneer* to a *smile*, which certainly modifies the meaning of the poem!

The now-famous conditions of Dickinson's life have contributed much to our interpretive uncertainties concerning her religious belief, yet even these facts are often misunderstood and misrepresented. Clichés about Dickinson abound: the morbid New England nun, the crazed woman in white, the neurotic and frustrated lover (both heterosexual and homosexual), the morbid dweller on death, the repressed daughter of a Puritan tyrant, the Romantic rebel against conventional Christianity. Each of these sensational but simplistic taglines has some element of truth, but none accurately depict the full depth and complexity of this superbly gifted poet.

We often forget that for many years Dickinson led a relatively conventional, if privileged, upper-middle-class life. She was born in 1830, and by the time she was a teenager, her father was a well-to-do lawyer with a prominent social position in the small Massachusetts town of Amherst (population 2,600) where she lived all of her life. Her grandfather had been one of the founders of the all-male Amherst College, and the annual College Commencement Day tea hosted by the Dickinsons each August, along with the yearly Cattle Show, were the two social highlights

9. Sewall, *The Life of Emily Dickinson*, 1:xii.

of Amherst life. In her teens and early twenties the red-haired, freckled Dickinson regularly went to parties, sent witty Valentines, joined college men on woodland walks and carriage rides, and attended Amherst's First Church twice on Sundays. Dickinson was unusually well educated for a nineteenth-century woman, studying for seven years at Amherst Academy and for another year at Mount Holyoke (roughly similar to a year of college). She followed a demanding course of study that included a remarkable amount of science: Latin, German, botany, geology, history, "mental philosophy," and geometry. When Edward Dickinson was elected as Massachusetts Representative to Congress in 1855, Emily (then twenty-four) and her younger sister, Vinnie, spent three weeks visiting their father in Washington, DC, followed by a two-week trip to Philadelphia.

However, during Emily's late twenties, her mother, Emily Norcross Dickinson, had a mysterious physical collapse, and Emily began spending more and more time at home, gradually withdrawing from the Amherst community scene, although never completely giving up social interactions. She still spent many evenings next door at the Evergreens, the elegant Italian-style home of her older brother, Austin, and his wife, Sue. However, it seems clear from a few letters written during the late 1850s that she suffered some kind of emotional crisis or depression. "I stagger as I write," she confided to a favorite uncle (Letter 335). This was also the period in which she began compiling the fascicles, transcribing earlier poems even as she was writing new ones at an astounding pace; recent estimates are that she composed 88 poems in 1861, 227 in 1862, 295 in 1863, and 98 in 1864.[10] Nonetheless, in 1860, when she turned thirty, she was still going to church, albeit more sporadically, and appearing at the annual Commencement Day tea.

During the last half of her life (Dickinson died in 1886 when she was 55), she had a number of intense friendships that were maintained primarily through letters, although they also included personal visits. She fell in love at least twice—once with a still-unidentified man to whom she referred as "Master," and later in life with the elderly Judge Otis Phillips Lord, to whom she wrote some rather explicit love letters. During her thirties, she made several new friends—including the prominent editor of the *Springfield Republican*, Samuel Bowles—went to Boston twice for several months to receive medical treatment for eye problems, and be-

10. Habegger, *My Wars*, 405.

came passionate about both Shakespeare and Thoreau. After her faithful Newfoundland, Carlo, died in 1866, she roamed less in the woods and, because of difficulties with domestic help, spent more time making bread and tending her garden. It was also during this period that she began exclusively to wear white and sometimes to turn visitors away, limiting her personal interactions to a selected few family members, friends, and neighborhood children. It's inaccurate to describe Dickinson as a total recluse; she merely became quite particular about whom she would see and when she would see them. (Poor Samuel Bowles never knew what to expect when he came to Amherst.) During the last sixteen years of her life, Dickinson saw fewer and fewer people, but continued an extensive and lively correspondence.

Vinnie described Emily's withdrawal from society as "only a happen," a gradual process with no instigating crisis: "finding the life with her books and nature so congenial, continued to live it, always seeing her chosen friends and doing her part for the happiness of others."[11] As the daughter of a wealthy lawyer, Emily did not need to marry, teach school, or desperately scramble to find something among the limited job opportunities available to women in her time. She had the freedom to stay at home, helping to run a household that was also well supplied with servants, and to concentrate her energies on reading, writing, thinking, and gardening. And so she did, becoming more and more reserved, erratically refusing at times to see even good friends, and refraining from social visits and church attendance.

Did Dickinson begin to suffer from agoraphobia or panic attacks? Did she withdraw from the world because she was disappointed in love? Was she unhealthily obsessed with death and loss, a victim of clinical depression? Did she deliberately seclude herself in order to devote her energies to writing? Did she find more freedom in her eccentric behavior than in following social conventions? Perhaps all of these explanations, to greater or lesser extents, contributed to Dickinson's uncommon life during her final sixteen years.

Pilgrim or Pagan?

One of the many mysteries of Emily Dickinson's life is the exact nature of her religious and spiritual commitments. Much like her contemporary

---

11. Sewell, *The Life of Emily Dickinson*, 1:153.

Herman Melville, Emily Dickinson apparently could neither believe nor be comfortable in her disbelief, as Nathaniel Hawthorne said about the author of *Moby-Dick*. In her letters, she often refers to herself as a "pagan," but she also talks about her life as a "pilgrimage." Several of her poems refer to the story of Jacob, who wrestled with God for a long agonizing night, ending up with both a blessing and a wound, and Dickinson seems to have identified with this biblical rebel. Unlike doubters today, Dickinson never questioned the fact that God existed, but she spent many hours wondering about God's nature. I think it is fair to say that she had an intense, but often troubled, relationship with God.

Certain facts about her religious life and background can be ascertained and provide helpful background for her poems that treat faith and doubt. Mid-nineteenth-century Amherst was predominantly a society of evangelical Congregationalists, neither rigorous Calvinist Puritans—like their ancestors—nor more liberal Unitarians—who had recently begun to dominate the Boston area. Amherst College had been founded in 1820 in reaction to Harvard Divinity School's embrace of Unitarianism, with a mission to fight the error of such false doctrines and to train clergy faithful to the Scriptures and the Reformation. Unlike the Puritan emphasis on God's judgment and human sinfulness, the Unitarian movement emphasized a beneficent but distant God and affirmed the basic goodness of the human heart. Jesus was viewed as an admirable teacher of love and peace, rather than as the Son of God, and the Bible was read as a collection of moral stories rather than as the inspired Word of God.

Despite its prominence in American literary history because of the influence of Ralph Waldo Emerson, Unitarianism was in reality a small movement. The major religious development during the first half of the nineteenth century was the unprecedented growth of evangelical Protestant Christianity, with evangelical churches—including Methodists, Baptists, Presbyterians, most Congregationalists, many Episcopalians, and Friends—making up at least 85 percent of American congregations in 1860. While salvation for the earlier Puritans was mediated through institutions such as the family and the church, for the newly emerging evangelicals, salvation was an unmediated, directly personal experience, often elicited through emotional revivals. The revival spirit crossed both theological and regional lines, affecting both Methodist camp meetings in the South and Calvinist colleges in New England. The evangelical Congregationalists of Amherst continued to hold to the doctrines of the

Reformation—including God's sovereignty, human sin, Christ's divinity and atoning death, and the need for personal salvation—but they, along with their Wesleyan and holiness counterparts, also increasingly emphasized revivalism.[12] Resisting the Unitarians' abandonment of belief in a biblical trinitarian God but also searching for something more than a dry, rational Enlightenment deism, the stolid farmers and merchants of the Connecticut River Valley experienced wave after wave of evangelical revival in the first half of the nineteenth century.

Dickinson grew up attending a Congregationalist church, hearing (and often discussing) sermons, participating in daily family devotions, attending public lectures on religious topics, talking about theology with young Amherst College men, and reading the Bible. The Dickinson Collection at Harvard University has nineteen Bibles from the Dickinson family, including an 1843 King James edition that belonged to Emily. Her father read a chapter a day aloud during family devotions, but Emily herself must have spent many hours poring through the Scriptures, judging by the wonderful range of biblical quotations and allusions infusing her poetry and letters. We will use the King James translation in our reflections on her poems so that we can notice these echoes. Richard B. Sewall says, "She was saturated with [the Bible] and could apparently summon it to her aid at will."[13] She ranged widely through both the Old and New Testaments, but some of her favorite passages were from Revelation (especially what she called "the Gem chapter," Revelation 21), Isaiah, I Corinthians, and the Gospels. As we will see, Dickinson's poetry is permeated with biblical language, images, allusions, quotations, and thought. She had a scriptural imagination, and her wrestling with God often took the form of poetically engaging with God's Word.

She also repeatedly struggled with a massive social pressure to undergo a conversion experience, refusing all of her life to make a formal profession of faith and join the church. Such reluctance was not that unusual in the nineteenth century. When Emily was young, the entire Dickinson family faithfully attended Amherst's First Church, even though Mrs. Dickinson was the only professing member. When the sacrament of Communion was observed at the end of the service, about once every three months, Emily and her older brother Austin would go

12. Noll, *America's God*, 170–73.
13. Sewell, *The Life of Emily Dickinson*, 2:694.

home with their father, while Mrs. Dickinson remained to participate in Communion. Edward Dickinson intellectually accepted and affirmed the truth of Christianity, but he had not gone through the required emotional experience of salvation. He was not alone. Nineteenth-century Congregational societies were made up of two overlapping groups: church and parish. Church members had undergone "conversion" and made a public profession of faith, while parish members were active in the life of the church—worshipping regularly, tithing, and exercising leadership over finances and hiring—excluded only from participating in Communion. The revival movements of the 1830s through 1850s were aimed at these non-communicants, attempting to produce the emotional experiences and convictions necessary for conversion.

When Dickinson was ten or eleven, she briefly believed that she had experienced such a conversion. A few years later she wrote a friend, "I can say that I never enjoyed such perfect peace and happiness as the short time in which I felt I had found my saviour. . . . It was then my greatest pleasure to commune alone with the great God & to feel that he would listen to my prayers." But the emotional high of this experience soon ebbed, and when another revival occurred in 1845, which resulted in forty-six confessions of faith, many among Amherst teenagers, Dickinson stayed away from the daily services, fearing she "was so easily excited that I might again be deceived." Nonetheless, she wrote her friend, "There is an aching void in my heart which I am convinced the world never can fill. . . . I continually hear Christ saying to me Daughter give me thine heart" (Letter 10).

This story reminds me of the experience of a friend who went to a Christian summer camp when he was in high school and went forward during the final bonfire appeal to "dedicate his life to Christ." When the next year's emotion-charged bonfire occurred, he went forward again, convinced that the first time didn't take. After four years of camp bonfires, he began to question the validity of such experiences, rebelling against Christianity in all its forms. But when he entered his twenties, he gradually began to think about Christian faith in a more nuanced way, as a continual process of growth even in the midst of doubts, as a commitment to faith even in the absence of high emotions.

Dickinson's early revival experience similarly made her wary of subsequent experiences. Two years later in 1847, while attending Mt. Holyoke, she again withstood a powerful revival movement that swept the school and the pressure exerted by many of her close friends. This time her resistance came not so much from a crisis of the intellect as from a failure to experience an intense emotion. Her cousin reported, "Emily Dickinson appears no different. I hoped I might have good news to write, with regard to her. She says she has no particular objection to becoming a Christian and . . . feels bad when she hears of one and another of her friends who are expressing a hope but still she feels no more interest."[14] How does one know when one truly is responding to the work of God and when one is succumbing to peer pressure or the ecstasies of a moment? How does one produce an emotional response when one is not forthcoming? With a woman as intelligent and passionate and honest as Dickinson, these were pressing questions.

In 1850, another revival took place in Amherst, with nightly meetings in the Amherst Academy building, and this time Edward, Vinnie, and Susan Gilbert (who was soon to marry Austin) were converted. Emily took a more openly defiant stance this time, writing a friend, "Christ is calling everyone here, all my companions have answered, even my darling Vinnie believes she loves, and trusts him, and I am standing alone in rebellion" (Letter 35). Austin made profession of faith in 1856, so when another revival occurred in 1857–58, during her period of emotional crisis, Emily was the only member of the Dickinson family who had not joined the church. She resisted again.

Nonetheless, she was unquestionably fascinated by the powerful New England tradition of sermonizing, commenting often in her letters on sermons and preachers. One scholar has conservatively estimated that Dickinson heard well over fifteen hundred sermons when she was regularly attending church, and the Dickinson family library contained many published collections of sermons.[15] Sermons with dry explications of doctrines bored her, but those with emotional intensity, vivid imagery, or verbal force particularly moved her. When the long-time minister of First Church retired, Emily joined in her father's outrage with the interim preacher (who apparently was of the "hell, fire, and brimstone" variety), expressing relief when the church brought in the Reverend Edward S. Dwight, who, she wrote, "preached beautifully" (Letter 140). In 1853 she heard the visiting Reverend Edwards Amasa Park preach a sermon about Judas that stayed with her for over twenty years: "I never heard anything

---

14. Habegger, *My Wars*, 203.

15. Doriani, *Emily Dickinson*, 45.

like it," she wrote Austin, "and dont [*sic*] expect to again till we stand at the great white throne. . . . And when it was all over, and that wonderful man sat down, people stared at each other, and looked as wan and wild, as if they had seen a spirit, and wondered they had not died. How I wish you had heard him" (Letter 142). During Dwight's tenure at First Church, which lasted until 1860, Emily even attended services alone at times, when the rest of the Dickinson family was out of town.

Yet another revival at First Church took place in 1873, so affecting Edward Dickinson that he recommitted his life to God in a written statement discovered after his death. This re-awakening also prompted in him a new concern for his wayward daughter, who by this point was no longer attending church services, so he asked the current minister of First Church, Reverend Jonathan Jenkins, to visit Emily to discuss her spiritual state. All we know of their interview is the fact that Rev. Jenkins afterward reported to Edward that "Miss Emily was 'sound.'"[16]

Despite never formally becoming a church member, Dickinson had a deep interest in religious and spiritual issues, frequently turning to ministers for conversation, correspondence, and counsel, as well as drawing on the Christian tradition to provide comfort and consolation to others. When Benjamin Newton, who four years earlier had been a law student in Edward Dickinson's office, died in 1853, Emily wrote to his minister to ask if Newton's faith remained strong on his deathbed, expressing a hope that he was now at home in heaven. Similarly, her troubles in the late 1850s prompted her to write the Reverend Charles Wadsworth, the pastor of the Arch Street Presbyterian Church in Philadelphia. She may have heard Wadsworth, who was a renowned but somber orator, preach during her visit to Philadelphia in 1855, and some scholars believe that Wadsworth may have been the unnamed "Master" with whom she fell in love (although there are several other candidates).

Throughout the 1860s and 1870s, as more and more of her family and friends died—her favorite aunt, her father, Samuel Bowles—Dickinson responded at times with anger and sarcasm about the existence of a loving God, and at other times with a simple confidence in God's care and love. When her mother died in 1882, she wrote, "I believe we shall in some manner be cherished by our Maker—that the One who gave us this remarkable earth has the power still farther to surprise that which He has

---

16. Jenkins, *Emily Dickinson*, 82.

caused. Beyond that all is silence" (Letter 785). But less than a year later, one of her most difficult trials came with the sudden death from typhoid of her eight-year-old nephew, Thomas Gilbert Dickinson, the youngest son of Austin and Sue. Gib, as the boy was called, was a charming, sunny, likable child, and his death shocked the entire family. The night he died, Emily paid a rare visit to the Evergreens, became nauseous from the smell of the disinfectants, went home with a severe headache, and took to her own sickbed for several weeks. She was haunted by Gib's delirious dying words, "Open the Door, open the Door, they are waiting for me," writing a friend, "*Who* were waiting for him, all we possess we would give to know—Anguish at last opened it, and he ran to the little Grave at his Grandparents' feet" (Letter 873).

Judging from the evidence of the poems and letters, on some days Emily doubted; on others, she believed. She speaks of such vacillations in one of the playful letters that she wrote to her late-life fiancé, Judge Otis Phillips Lord: "On subjects of which we know nothing, or should I say *Beings*—is 'Phil' [Judge Lord] a 'Being' or a 'Theme,' we both believe and disbelieve a hundred times an Hour, which keeps Believing nimble" (Letter 750). Who hasn't experienced similar confused feelings regarding faith and doubt? Perhaps we should not try to render a final verdict on Emily Dickinson's relationship with God and instead trust that the two of them are working out their differences even now.

The Publication of the Poems

During her lifetime, Emily Dickinson did not try to have her poems published in a public forum. Her poetry was a private realm, one that she shared with close friends and family, but not with the world at large. The construction of poetry as a product, a means of making money, was only just beginning to take root in nineteenth-century America, and many conservative Americans believed that the best kind of writing circulated only in private. If you were lucky enough to know Emily Dickinson, it was not unusual for her to send you a poem enclosed in a letter, or else simply to send you a poem, sometimes with a flower or a loaf of bread. Several hundred of her poems were included with her correspondence or sent to people's homes, "a vital part of the commerce of friendship," as her recent biographer, Alfred Habegger, puts it.[17] She often used her poetic

17. Habegger, *My Wars*, 354.

art as a way to offer consolation to those who were sick or mourning; if you had suffered a loss, instead of a Hallmark card, you might receive a Dickinson gem. Offering such poetic gifts thus functioned as a ministry. Other times, her poems might offer a humorous commentary on some event or idea, or an account of a natural phenomenon, such as sunset, a snake, a flower, or a hummingbird. She occasionally sent the same poem to different people, often with a few changes, which is one reason for some of the different versions, or variant readings, of several poems.

Her sister-in-law, Sue Gilbert Dickinson; two cousins, Louise and Francis Norcross; and Samuel Bowles were among some of the most frequent recipients of poems. Another important friend was Thomas Wentworth Higginson, whose *Atlantic Monthly* essay giving advice for would-be writers prompted her to initiate a correspondence. Higginson was a former Unitarian minister who gave up the pulpit to work as a writer, lecturer, and abolitionist. Dickinson turned to him primarily as a literary consultant, sending him some of her poems for his assessment: "Are you too deeply occupied to say if my Verse is alive?" she wrote in her first letter, sent in April of 1863 (Letter 260). Higginson apparently found her poetry too unconventional and urged her to employ a more regular meter and syntax—advice that she completely ignored. Nonetheless, they continued to correspond until her death, and she sent him over one hundred poems over their twenty-two-year friendship.

Ten of her poems were published in Dickinson's lifetime, but it's doubtful that she gave permission for any of them to appear, and she was not publicly identified as their author. Recipients of her poems often showed them to other people, who may have submitted them for publication. For example, in 1858, "Nobody knows this little rose" (Poem 11) appeared in the *Springfield Republican*, with the heading: "To Mrs. _____, with a Rose [Surreptitiously communicated to the *Republican*.]" Several people attempted at various points to persuade Dickinson to allow them to publish her work, but she refused.

Obviously her family knew she wrote poetry; however, when Dickinson died in 1886 (of Bright's Disease according to her death certificate), Vinnie was stunned to discover a huge collection of poems and letters in a locked drawer in Dickinson's room. More than eight hundred poems were carefully copied into forty fascicles. Another four hundred poems were in ten unbound sets, and there were hundreds of poems in fair copies, semi-final drafts, and early drafts written on scraps of paper, the backs of envelopes, and edges of newspapers. Vinnie apparently had no idea how prolific a poet her sister had been. Following Emily's directions, Vinnie destroyed all of the letters, but she could not bring herself to burn the poems; instead, she asked Sue to select and prepare a collection for publication. After two years, Sue had made little progress, so Vinnie retrieved the manuscripts and asked Mabel Loomis Todd, the wife of an Amherst professor, to take over the editorial job. Todd toiled faithfully to decipher Emily's difficult handwriting, eventually selecting and editing several hundred poems that appeared in 1890 as *Poems by Emily Dickinson*, working with the support and assistance of Higginson. A laudatory review by William Dean Howells in the influential *Harper's Monthly* followed, and the book quickly went through several editions.

A family saga of soap-opera proportion was brewing, however. A few years before Emily's death, Mabel Todd had begun an affair with Austin Dickinson. Vinnie's turning over of Emily's poetry to Todd, then, was a double betrayal for Sue. When Austin died in 1895, a series of legal battles resulted in the eventual division of the poetic manuscripts between Susan Dickinson and Mabel Todd. What the Amherst neighbors called "The War between the Houses," resulted in a series of competing editions of Dickinson's poems and letters, as well as biographical interpretations. All of these early editions tidied up Dickinson's unconventional verse—removing capital letters and dashes, changing puzzling words—in order to make it adhere more closely to the poetic norms of the period.

It was not until 1955 that Thomas H. Johnson produced the first complete scholarly edition of Dickinson's poems working from the original manuscripts and preserving the original capitalization, punctuation, and spelling. The manuscripts once controlled by Sue and Vinnie are now housed at Harvard University, while Mabel Todd's portion eventually became the property of the Amherst College Library. Dickinson did not give her poems titles, but we now commonly refer to them by means of a number assigned by one of her twentieth-century editors. Johnson was the first to use this numbering system, putting the poems into a rough chronological order. However, in 1999 a new scholarly edition of Dickinson's poetry was published, edited by Robert W. Franklin, which is now considered a better, more reliable edition. Franklin has re-dated and re-edited many of the poems, so the numbers he assigns to the poems are different. The poems reprinted in this book, for the most part, are from Franklin's edition, and are indicated with an F. However, I have also included the Johnson number, indicated with a J, as this number may be more familiar to you if you read Dickinson before 1999, or have an older copy of her poems.

While such technical matters may seem unimportant, editorial choices contribute to the open-endedness of Dickinson's poetry. As we have seen, she herself left some decisions unresolved, refusing to decide upon a single word, sending alternative versions of poems to different people. Her editors have, at times, interpreted her handwriting or the dating of her poetry differently, or made other editorial choices that contribute to a poem's meaning. We need look no further than the poem that gives us the title for this book of meditations to see the difference one single letter can make. Previously I used Johnson's version (Poem 1442J), but here is how Franklin's version reads:

> To mend each tattered Faith
> There is a needle fair
> Though no appearance indicate –
> 'Tis threaded in the Air –
>
> And though it do not wear
> As if it never Tore
> 'Tis very comfortable indeed
> And *specious* as before – (#1468F, italics mine)

There's a big difference between a mended faith being "spacious" and "specious"—false, hollow, or erroneous. I have looked at a microfilm copy of the original poem in Dickinson's handwriting, and she clearly wrote "specious," but that kind of sarcasm does not seem to fit with the tone of the rest of the poem. Is it possible that she misspelled the word? Did Johnson deliberately choose to use "spacious"? Could the garment of faith be both comfortable and specious?

"To mend each tattered Faith" epitomizes the difficulties in determining Emily Dickinson's intentions for her poetry. But it also—in either of its versions—gives us much to ponder as we attempt to listen for God and explore our experiences and responses.

Devotion 1

Poem 90F (140J)

An altered look about the hills –
A Tyrian light the village fills –
A wider sunrise in the morn –
A deeper twilight on the lawn –
A print of a vermillion foot –
A purple finger on the slope –
A flippant fly opon the pane –
A spider at his trade again –
An added strut in Chanticleer –
A flower expected everywhere –
An axe shrill singing in the woods –
Fern odors on untravelled roads –
All this and more I cannot tell –
A furtive look you know as well –
And Nicodemus' Mystery
Receives it's annual reply!

*Consider: What is the relationship of the coming of spring and Nicodemus'
question in John 3, "How can a person be born again?"*

Contrary to our common stereotypes, many scientists believe in God.
In fact, surveys demonstrate that among American academics, natural
scientists make up the greatest percentage of Christian believers. People
who study the humanities—literature, music, art, philosophy—make

up the second largest group, with the social scientists bringing up the rear. (Ironically, these surveys are conducted by social scientists.) There's something about the intricacies and mysteries of the natural world that affirms and sometimes leads to faith. Attentive observers, those who take the time to study and describe the natural world, are often amazed and awe-struck at what they see.

This poem helps us take the time to see the incremental changes that occur with the arrival of spring. It does not follow Dickinson's more typical poetic form of quatrain divisions (four-verse lines), but instead falls into couplets, two sequential lines linked by rhyme, each of which includes a complete thought. Not until we reach the final couplet do we find a run-on line, in which the thought continues from the first half of the couplet into the second. The effect is to prompt us to read each line, pause, and mentally add another piece to the slowly emerging picture.

The initial three words, "An altered look," announce that the poem will describe change, but they also anticipate the poem's spiritual conclusion in a pun: the hills look like an altar, a place of worship. When we remember that an altar is a raised structure, often a flat-topped rock or table of wood or stone, the appropriateness of the pun becomes even more apparent. "I will lift up mine eyes unto the hills," the Psalmist sings, "from whence cometh my help" (121:1). The poem's opening line calls our attention to the slight changes in the appearance of the hills, perhaps the dead grass is greening, perhaps the light reflects differently.

From the hills our gaze moves down to the village, which is filled with "A Tyrian light." As the days grow steadily longer and the sun moves to the northern part of the sky, the quality of light also changes. *Tyrian* alludes to the ancient Mediterranean city of Tyre, and there is a deep rich purple color tinged with crimson that is called *Tyrian purple*. With this description, a prosaic New England village is transformed into an exotic seaport. Everything becomes enlarged: the sunrise becomes "wider" and the twilight "deeper." Lines five and six introduce the presence of some kind of being with a "vermillion foot" and a "purple finger," both of which leave their "print" upon the natural world. The royal shades (vermillion, not plain old red) refer back to the Tyrian light and evoke the hand of God at work. Just as God gave Moses two tables of stone "written with the finger of God," so the signs of spring are a testimony of God.

The tone of the poem shifts from awe to frivolity when we begin to observe the inhabitants of the natural world. The personification contributes to the sprightly feel, with the "flippant fly," the spider working hard "at his trade," and Chanticleer strutting about the farmyard. Even the homely rooster has become grander, endowed with a fairy tale name. Flowers are expected to arrive shortly, like guests at a train station, and there is "An axe shrill singing in the woods." It's curious that this axe is the only indication of human activity, which makes me wonder if it might metaphorically refer to a woodpecker hammering a tree. The fresh smell of spring comes from "fern odors on untravelled roads." (If those roads are untravelled, how did that person with the axe arrive in the woods? It has to be a bird!)

The cataloging of spring transformations concludes in line 13's admission that the poem has only scratched the surface of the manifold changes underway: "All this and more I cannot tell." The "look" named in the first line of the poem now is described as "furtive," done in a way that is intended to escape notice. The changes are subtle, but one who looks carefully, pays attention, can see them. The poet graciously says that I know this as well as she does, but if I am honest, I must admit that I need her assistance. I don't often stop to look carefully at or precisely name the minutia of nature. For this, I need her assistance.

The final couplet sums up what the transformations of spring reveal: the answer to "Nicodemus' Mystery." John relates the story of the inquisitive Pharisee named Nicodemus who secretly came to talk with Jesus in the darkness of the night. When Jesus tells him, "Except a man be born again, he cannot see the kingdom of God," Nicodemus replies, "How can a man be born when he is old? Can he enter the second time into his mother's womb, and be born?" (John 3:3–4). The mystery of spiritual regeneration is similar to the mystery of natural regeneration. The coming of spring doesn't *explain* spiritual rebirth: comprehending the scientific details of the movement of the sun, the effect of longer periods of light upon flora and fauna, the annual cycle of germination, etc., doesn't fully explain the miracle of spring. It's more that the one reminds us of the other, the annual rebirth of the world promises that we, too, can be born again.

Devotion 2

Poem 114F (112J)

Where bells no more affright the morn –
Where scrabble never comes –
Where very nimble Gentlemen
Are forced to keep their rooms –

Where tired Children placid sleep
Thro' centuries of noon
This place is Bliss – this town is Heaven –
Please, Pater, pretty soon!

"Oh could we climb where Moses stood,
And view the Landscape o'er"
Not Father's bells – nor Factories –
Could scare us any more!

Consider: How is the "town" of heaven described?

Since I am a night owl, preferring to go to bed after midnight and get up
after ten, I am particularly fond of this poem, which imagines heaven as
a place where we all get to sleep in. The poetic device of *anaphora*—using
the same word or phrase at the beginning of several successive lines—
highlights the poem's topic. In Dickinson's typical quatrain stanzas, it describes a place, "where" certain things either do or do not occur. The word

Heaven appears in line 7 and divides the poem into two halves: the first describing heaven and the second taking the form of a prayer of longing.

In an implied dramatic scene, a "very nimble Gentleman" rises early and rings a bell, rousing his household and calling them to begin their daily toil. The "tired Children" drag themselves out of bed and "scrabble"—grope around frantically in an effort to get dressed, prepare breakfast, and begin their chores. In Heaven, however, the scene will be reversed; no bells will "affright the morn," and such frantic scrabbling will not occur. The overly enthusiastic gentleman, who is clearly a morning lark, will be forced to stay in his room like a naughty child. And those poor weary children will "placid sleep" through "centuries of noon," an odd phrase that tells us that we are out of normal time and in eternity, a noon that lasts for hundreds of years. "This place is Bliss," the poet states straightforwardly, and those of us who love to sleep until noon and wish that our frantic lives allowed more time for peace and rest would agree.

In the second half of the poem, the speaker prays, "Please, Pater, pretty soon!" I long to find rest, for my burden and my eyelids are heavy. The use of the Latin word for *father* not only allows for a child-like alliteration (pretty please!) but also distinguishes the heavenly Father from the earthly "Father" of line eleven, with his demanding bells.

The poem is in perfect common meter, with fairly regular end rhymes (*comes/rooms, noon/soon, o'er/more*), and the appropriateness of its precise form becomes apparent when we reach the final stanza's quotation of two lines from Isaac Watt's hymn "There is a land of pure delight":

> Could we but climb where Moses stood,
> And view the landscape o'er,
> Not Jordan's stream, nor death's cold flood
> Should fright us from the shore.

This popular nineteenth-century hymn anticipates and yearns for heaven, the land of pure delight, referring to the story of Moses' glimpse of the promised land of Canaan from the top of Mt. Nebo as providing a type of our own glimpse of the heaven that is to come. In the system of biblical typology employed by Isaac Watts and generations of believers, the land of Canaan represents and foreshadows the promised land of heaven. Dickinson concludes her own hymn-poem by playfully paraphrasing Watts. The hymn advises that the sight of heaven would forestall any fear we might have of passing through death, represented in the water imagery. The hymnist's specific naming of "Jordan's stream" is replaced by the father's domestic bells while the more general description of "death's cold flood" is transformed into a factory bell, which sounds throughout an entire town, calling everyone to work. (During Dickinson's time, two straw-hat factories were located in downtown Amherst, and their steam whistles sounded at 6:00 a.m., 6:50 a.m., and 7:00 a.m.) Watts' final "Should fright us from the shore" becomes the more lighthearted "Could scare us any more!" although his "fright" is echoed in the first line of the poem.

In its wit and playfulness, Poem 114 brings us to the top of our own Mt. Nebo. According to Dickinson's final stanza, if we could see just a bit of heaven, the bells and scrabble of this life will no longer overwhelm us. And in reading and laughing about this poem, we may catch that glimpse.

Devotion 3

Poem 122F (130J)

These are the days when Birds come back –
A very few – a Bird or two –
To take a backward look.

These are the days when skies resume
The old – old sophistries of June –
A blue and gold mistake.

Oh fraud that cannot cheat the Bee.
Almost thy plausibility
Induces my belief,

Till ranks of seeds their witness bear –
And softly thro' the altered air
Hurries a timid leaf.

Oh sacrament of summer days,
Oh Last Communion in the Haze –
Permit a child to join –

Thy sacred emblems to partake –
They consecrated bread to take
And thine immortal wine!

Consider: How do you feel when you participate in the sacrament of Communion?

Another account of a season in nature, this poem describes a phenomenon occurring only in certain parts of the United States, both in Dickinson's New England and in the Pacific Northwest, where I live. If you live in the northern part of the world, you might have experienced it, too. When I was growing up, we called it *Indian summer*, a period of mild sunny weather often occurring in late October after summer appears to be over. September might have been cold and rainy, but then suddenly you are blessed with a week of warm, dry, beautiful weather. Although the origins of the phrase are uncertain, it is usually attributed to the fact that the phenomenon was first noticed in the eighteenth century in the parts of northeastern America where Native Americans were still living.

Dickinson describes Indian summer in three-line stanzas using language of belief and doubt. The emphatic "These are the days," repeated twice, employs a meter that strays from the iambic rhythm of most of the poem. The emphasis indicates the poem's subject. This might be seen as a riddle-poem. What are these days being described? Listen carefully for the clues. The first is that it is a time when "Birds come back," which sounds like spring, except for the fact that only "A very few – a Bird or two" return, and they are looking "backward," our first hint that this is a time after spring. Clue number two is the blue sky and golden sunlight that resemble nothing so much as a June day. So perhaps it is summer. But the skies "resume," or take on again, this appearance, which is then described as a "mistake." The "old – old sophistries of June" also indicates the deceptive nature of these appearances. A *sophistry* is a method of argumentation that appears very clever but is actually flawed or dishonest. The word comes from a Greek school of philosophers called the Sophists, who lived and argued (with Plato, among others) back in the fifth century BC. So such deceptions are very old. The repetition of *old*, with the dash, and the assonance of the long *o* sounds makes us linger on this line, just as summer lingers in the autumn.

But reality comes rushing in with the lament "Oh fraud that cannot cheat the Bee." The *o* sound appears again, only to lead into the harsh accusation of fraud in the iambic beat. The Bee, however, is not fooled; it has already piled up its winter stores of nectar and begun to hibernate. Once frost comes, bees sleep for almost ten months until the coming of the true spring. Nonetheless, the fraud or sophistry is so convincing that the speaker is almost convinced that summer has returned; her "belief" has almost been induced.

We've reached the center and turning point in the poem, which occurs with the signal "Till." For when "ranks of seeds their witness bear" and the leaves slowly and softly begin to fall, the true season becomes apparent. The air is "altered" like the hills in the spring time of Poem 90, and the pun again brings us to a religious altar: the Communion table. The mournful *Oh* in line 7 turns into a celebratory *Oh* in lines 13 and 14, as the poet rejoices in the "sacrament of summer days" and the "Last Communion in the Haze."

Indian summer re-enacts and re-members the true summer; it is a commemorative celebration that the poet asks, as a person of child-like faith, to be permitted to join. While partaking of the elements of the sacrament, the "sacred emblems" of "consecrated bread" and "immortal wine," we rejoice in the life of the summer even in the midst of the death of autumn, the blowing seeds and falling leaves. Yet the "witness" of the ranks, or multitudes, of seeds speaks not only of death but also of the new life to come. "Except a corn of wheat fall into the ground and die, it abideth alone: but if it die, it bringeth forth much fruit" (John 12:24).

In Rite 2, Eucharistic Prayer B, in *The Book of Common Prayer*, the celebrant opens the consecration of the elements with the following words: "And we offer our sacrifice of praise and thanksgiving to you, O Lord of all; presenting to you, from your creation, this bread and this wine." The bread that we eat has been made from those grains of wheat that fell into the ground and died. The wine that we drink is the fruit of the vine that dies back each winter only to be renewed again each spring. The emblems from God's creation both symbolize and embody the truth.

Devotion 4

Poem 151F (61J)

Papa above!
Regard a mouse
O'erpowered by the Cat!
Reserve within thy kingdom
A "Mansion" for the Rat!

Snug in seraphic Cupboards
To nibble all the day,
While unsuspecting Cycles
Wheel solemnly away!

Consider: Would you call God "Papa"? Why or why not?

"Our Father, which art in heaven, Hallowed be thy name," is how Jesus teaches us to pray in Matt 6:9. But that is excessively grand language to use when we are feeling small and insignificant. In this lighthearted version of the Lord's Prayer, we address God with the more intimate "Papa," just as Jesus affectionately and startlingly called him "Abba," or Daddy. This is the language of a child, simple and straightforward, personal and familiar—both as in relating to the family and as easily recognized. The odd position of the poem's opening two words, removed from the subsequent quatrain pattern, literally puts the Papa "above" the rest of the poem.

The childlike tone continues in the plea to pay attention to the mouse that is being overcome, and perhaps eaten, by a cat, a concrete domestic instance of a plea to "deliver us from evil." The "O'erpowered" contains a faint echo of "For thine is the kingdom, and the power, and the glory," with the kingdom appearing in line 4. This line from the Lord's Prayer especially fascinated Dickinson, and she refers to it in several letters. In the poem's first stanza, the Papa-God is asked to do two things: "Regard" and "Reserve." See our plight, the poet pleads, besieged by enemies. Reserve for us a "Mansion"; the quotation marks alert us to the fact that this word is both a quotation and ironic. "In my Father's house are many mansions," Jesus assures his disciplines in John 14:2, "if it were not so, I would have told you." But the idea of a mansion for a rat (which the mouse has become in order to create a perfect rhyme of the kind Dr. Seuss would approve) is a bit silly.

I'd be happy with a mere cupboard, the poet says, albeit it a "seraphic" one. A seraph is a high-ranking angel, so this is a heavenly cupboard. To be snuggly hidden away from the terrors of the cat and "nibble all the day" would be a cozy provision of "our daily bread." Instead of being eaten by the cat, the Mouse will eat heavenly food and "hunger no more" (Rev 7:16).

Even the lowly, the childlike, and the small will find a place in heaven. We will enter a comfortable home where evil does not threaten and all our wants are met. The intimate domesticity of this picture of heaven stands in sharp contrast with the huge impersonal forces of the universe described in the final two lines. The "Cycles" are "unsuspecting," oblivious to the nibbling mouse safely ensconced in her cupboard as they "Wheel solemnly away." There's a mechanistic quality to this repetitive process, like the wheel of fate turning over and over. Such cold indifference is all that some people are able to see in the universe, but this endlessly repeating cycle of time is also a description of eternity, which the mouse will happily spend in her snug seraphic cupboard. On those days when I am feeling like a besieged mouse, I need to turn to my Papa above.

Devotion 5

Poem 207F (214J)

I taste a liquor never brewed –
From Tankards scooped in Pearl –
Not all the Frankfort Berries
Yield such an Alcohol!

Inebriate of air – am I –
And Debauchee of Dew –
Reeling – thro' endless summer days –
From inns of molten Blue –

When "Landlords" turn the drunken Bee
Out of the Foxglove's door –
When Butterflies – renounce their "drams" –
I shall but drink the more!

Till Seraphs swing their snowy Hats –
And Saints – to windows run –
To see the little Tippler
Leaning against the – Sun!

Consider: Have you ever felt drunk on the beauty of nature? When?

With its unexpected picture of a carousing Dickinson and its ecstatic reveling in the long days of summer, this may be my favorite Dickinson poem. Like one hundred and forty other poems by Dickinson, Poem 207 opens with the centering personal pronoun "I," in which we are invited to find ourselves as we read. When the words of this poem reverberate in my head or resound from my mouth, I participate in its celebration of summer and faith.

The deceptively straightforward first line poses a riddle: what kind of liquor has not been brewed? This mysterious brew is drunk from elegant "Tankards" lined "in Pearl," and its quality surpasses even the exquisite beer brewed from German hops ("Frankfort berries"). In an alternative wording in her fascicle copy, Dickinson offers line 3 as, "Not all the Vats opon [*sic*] the Rhine," alluding again to German beer brewing. This poem was one of the few that appeared in print during Dickinson's lifetime, published in the *Springfield Daily Republican* on May 4, 1861, under the title of "The May-Wine," a title assigned by an editor, not by Dickinson. The Rhine region is also renowned for its sweet white wines, but "Tankard" and the generally rollicking tone more strongly suggest that the liquor in question is beer.

The riddle is sustained until the second stanza exposes the poem's controlling metaphor; Dickinson is drunk on nature, inebriated on air, debauched on dew. Perhaps her Tankard is a white lily, one of Dickinson's favorite flowers. This vessel is concrete and earthy (it's not a fine-stemmed crystal goblet). While we can figure out the meaning of "*Debauchee* of Dew," because of its resemblance to the word *debauched*, the noun form is quite curious, appearing primarily in late-seventeenth and eighteenth-century British prose. A *Debauchee*, the *Oxford English Dictionary* tells us, is "one who is addicted to vicious indulgence in sensual pleasure." Although the connotations of addiction, indulgence, and sensual pleasure ring true, it's hard to take the suggestion of viciousness too seriously when it is applied to the drinking of dew.

However, after merely tasting the beer (or wine) in the first line, we swiftly become intoxicated, "Reeling – thro' endless summer days." Tankards do hold a considerable volume of liquor! We seem to be on a pub crawl, staggering from inn to inn. The metaphoric inns in which we drink are painted molten blue, the color of the summer sky, but the adjective *molten* also evokes the idea of liquid heat, both an alcoholic drink and a humid summer day.

The opening noun of stanza two, *Inebriate,* is paired structurally, alphabetically, and grammatically with the poem's opening pronoun, *I.* The first two stanzas thus focus on a person—the one who drinks—but the third and fourth stanzas shift our attention to the passing of time, with their respective openings of *When* and *Till*. When closing time arrives, the "Landlords" of the drinking establishments ask their patrons to leave; in one case kicking a "drunken Bee" out the door of the Foxglove Inn, perhaps with the arrival of fall. The more refined "Butterflies" voluntarily give up their drams, small glasses of cordials or spirituous liquors, perhaps by taking a nineteenth-century temperance pledge. But neither closing hours nor social disapproval will cause Dickinson to stop imbibing.

The future indicated by "I *shall* but drink the more!" extends until the events of the closing stanza, when "Saints" and "Seraphs" welcome the poet to a place that we slowly recognize as heaven. The angels swing their snow-white hats in greeting while the saints run to the windows of the heavenly mansion to gaze upon "the little Tippler," who unsteadily advances, "Leaning against the – Sun!" as she is too drunk to navigate herself. Set off with Dickinson's characteristic dash, capitalization, and exclamation point, the ultimate word of the poem simultaneously concludes the celebration of the magnificent days of summer and posits the sustaining role of Jesus, the Son. Summer days, despite appearances, are not endless; the celebratory "snowy" hats also quietly allude to the fact that winter will come. Yet this song of the drunken belle of Amherst reminds us that the beauties of summer are truly glorious—leading to the glory of the Son/Sun.

Devotion 6

Poem 252F (237J)

I think just how my shape will rise –
When I shall be *"forgiven"* –
Till Hair – and Eyes –and timid Head –
Are *out of sight* – in Heaven –

I think just how my lips will weigh –
With shapeless –quivering – prayer –
That you – *so late* – *"consider" me* –
The *"sparrow"* of your care –

I mind me that of Anguish –sent –
Some drifts were moved away –
Before my simple bosom – broke –
And why not *this* – if *they*?

And so I con that thing – *"forgiven"* –
Until – delirious – borne –
By my long bright – and *longer* – trust –
I *drop* my Heart – *unshriven*!

Consider: What do you think it means to be forgiven by God?

In this dash-riddled poem, we watch the poet as she struggles with what it means to be forgiven, and, if we pronounce the "I," we enact the difficult thought process ourselves. The opening phrase of each stanza announces the act of reflection: "I think," "I think," and "I mind." The final stanza concludes, "And so I con that thing – '*forgiven*'." To *con* is to study with care and close attention, or to learn or memorize something. This poem examines the word *forgiven*, doubly emphasized with both italics and quotation marks, but concludes with the rhyming antonym *unshriven,* the state of not having confessed sins or having received absolution.

In the first stanza, the reflection concerns the physical ascension of the body to heaven, "how my shape will rise." The use of the future tense "shall be" in line 2 indicates that the state of forgiveness has not yet happened. This is a "what if" exploration. Specific parts of the body—hair, eyes, and head—will rise until the poet is moved out of earthly sight into Heaven. Forgiveness will include the resurrection of the body and a new realm of life.

Forgiveness will also involve prayer. The description of the prayer as "shapeless" and "quivering" suggests uncertainty and fear, and the heaviness of the lips described in line 5 implies reluctance or difficulty in speaking. We might think this timidity arises from a broken and contrite heart, but when the poet turns to address God in lines 7 and 8, we find an odd combination of anger and confidence. If she were to be forgiven, the poet is confident that God would watch over her. The quoted words "consider" and "sparrow" both compactly refer to instances in which Christ assured his followers that they had nothing to fear, that God would be with them. "Consider the lilies of the field," Jesus says in the Sermon on the Mount, "how they grow; they toil not, neither do they spin: And yet I say unto you, That even Solomon in all his glory was not arrayed like one of these. . . . Therefore take no thought, saying, What shall we eat? Or What shall we drink? . . . for your heavenly Father knoweth that ye have need of all these things" (Matt 6:28–32). Similarly, in Matthew 10, Jesus tells his disciples that even as God watches over the sparrow worth half a farthing, so He will watch over them. Despite the fact that these quotes evoke God's care, the poetic voice is angry that God regards her as one of His creatures "*so late*"—now but not earlier.

Why does the action verb change from "think" to "mind" in the third stanza? To the element of thought, "minding" adds the connotation of watching to avoid danger, as well as objecting or being bothered. "Mind the gap," the London Tube advises departing passengers; "I mind his rudeness," we might say. It could also be an abbreviated version of "remind," a common American regional usage. And so the poet remembers that/ objects to/watches as "*Some*" of her "Anguish" is taken away to prevent her from completely collapsing, but not all of the pain. She protests, "why not *this* – if *they*?"

She has now articulated two complaints against God: 1) why didn't you begin watching over me sooner? and, 2) why haven't you taken away all my suffering? Perhaps you share one or both of these complaints. David certainly did, "Why standest thou afar off, O Lord?" he questions in Psalm 10, "why hidest thou thyself in times of trouble?" (1). I wonder, though, if this poem confuses care and action. While I have never doubted that God cares for me, that God has always numbered the hairs of my head and that I have always been one of God's sparrows, there have been occasions when I wished that God would insert Himself into the action. In Jesus' account of the sparrow, God does not stop the bird from falling on the ground; rather God is with the bird as it falls. I want God to catch me. And for some mysterious but sovereign reason that I do not pretend to fully comprehend or accept, sometimes I fall.

In the last stanza of the poem, the result of this exploration of forgiveness appears to be a rejection of God. The poet drops her heart, in contrast to the rising shape of the first line of the poem, and the final word is the ominous *unshriven*. The problem of pain prevents her from confessing and accepting forgiveness. Yet the tortured syntax and contradictions of lines 14 and 15 suggest a delirium produced by too much thought: "Until – delirious –borne - / By my long bright – and *longer – trust –*." The description of trust is positive: it endures, stretches out, is illuminated; it may even be a trust that yearns, or longs for. Borne, or carried by such trust, we drop our Heart? Or is our delirium produced, birthed, by our trust? However, *delirious* and *drop* are linked through alliteration, which may suggest that letting go of our faith is an act of confusion caused by injury.

I can't ultimately figure out this poem and read it in such a way as to make consistent sense. But I do know that some of its painful questions echo questions I have felt. I understand the anguish and the anger.

Devotion 7

Poem 373F (501J)

This World is not conclusion.
A Species stands beyond –
Invisible, as Music –
But positive, as Sound –
It beckons, and it baffles –
Philosophy, dont know –
And through a Riddle, at the last –
Sagacity, must go –
To guess it, puzzles scholars –
To gain it, Men have borne
Contempt of Generations
And Crucifixion, shown –
Faith slips – and laughs, and rallies –
Blushes, if any see –
Plucks at a twig of Evidence –
And asks a Vane, the way –
Much Gesture, from the Pulpit –
Strong Hallelujahs roll –
Narcotics cannot still the Tooth
That nibbles at the soul –

Consider: How is faith is described in this poem? Does your faith some-times look like this? When and why?

From a confident assertion in the simple declarative sentence of the first line, to the nagging "Tooth" of uncertainty nibbling at the soul in the final line, Emily Dickinson runs the gamut of faith and doubt in this poem, as many of us do in a single day, much less a life. Despite the implication of quatrains by means of the x/a/x/a rhyme, the poem relentlessly progresses through a train of thoughts, emotions, and moods without any stanza breaks.

The opening affirmation that "This World" is *not* all there is, period, is immediately followed by several analogies. Just as we know that *Sound* is a real phenomena, despite our inability to see or touch *Music*, so we know that some form of life, or *Species*, exists after death. Botanically, *species* refers to the specific characteristics of a plant, as opposed to the broad category indicated by *genus*. In a literal pun, the sounds of the poem embody this reality, too; the *s* opening and closing *Species* and *stands* is subsequently more subtly embedded in *invisible* and *music* before overtly and positively appearing once more in *Sound*.

In line 5, our uncertainty about the exact nature of this new Species is captured in the vague pronoun *It*, which occurs again in lines 9 and 10. The unknown form of life, immortality, both "beckons" invitingly as well as "baffles" our attempts at explanation. Such explanatory efforts make up "Philosophy," which "dont know," for despite logical or scientific attempts to describe what lies beyond mortal life, it is only when one passes through the "Riddle" of death that one can "know" this unfamiliar Species. Even the ultimate personification of wisdom, "Sagacity," must go through the Riddle. The one syllable words "must go" and the straightforward perfect rhyme of "go/know" emphasize the inevitability of this process, contrasted with the more complex diction of "Sagacity." Even "scholars" are puzzled and can only "guess it."

Despite the intellectual failures depicted in terms such as *baffles*, *Riddle*, *guess*, *puzzles*, we return briefly in the middle of the poem to the testimony of faith provided in history: Men have borne "Contempt" and "Crucifixion" in order to achieve immortality: "To gain it." But all too quickly our confidence is again shaken, as "Faith"—personified as a silly little girl—"slips – and laughs, and rallies - / Blushes, if any see," and then desperately attempts to find physical evidence in such ridiculous sources as a thin "twig of Evidence" or a changeable weathervane. The stumbling gait created by the dashes in line 13 further suggests the lack of sure footing.

The closing quatrain turns to one more potential source for answers to this puzzle—the church. But Dickinson finds little comfort there. The frantically gesturing minister described in line 17 is structurally and visually too close to a whirling weathervane to provide "the way," while the "Strong Hallelujahs" arising from the fervent congregation are equally unconvincing. We almost enter into the emotional experience of an old-time revival meeting as the poem concludes with extreme sights and sounds, "much" gesturing and "Strong" verbal responses. And for restrained and cerebral Christians (or moods), nothing can be more off-putting or even faith-quelling than such extreme emotional outbursts.

Neither Emotions nor Evidence provide complete answers to the mystery of life after death. Yet people in the nineteenth century, just as today, frequently tried to convince themselves of their faith either through emotional extremes (evangelical revivals) or philosophical proof (Scottish Common Sense Realism). Neither, this poem reminds us, can completely "still the Tooth" of doubt; both serve merely as "Narcotics" that might momentarily numb pain but will not address the root problem. The wonderful word "nibbles," however, reminds us that our small gentle bites of doubt need not be fatal to our souls. Faith, after all, is "the evidence of things not seen" (Heb 11:1). According to her niece, Dickinson once said of the Apostle Thomas, "his faith in anatomy was stronger than his faith in faith."[1] Having faith in faith—now that's the challenge.

---

1. Bianchi, *The Life and Letters*, 99.

Devotion 8

Poem 377F (502J)

At least – to pray – is left – is left –
Oh Jesus – in the Air –
I know not which thy chamber is –
I'm knocking – everywhere –

Thou settest Earthquake in the South –
And Maelstrom, in the Sea –
Say, Jesus Christ of Nazareth –
Hast thou no arm for Me?

Consider: Under what kinds of circumstances do you pray?

Another of Dickinson's poems *about* prayer, this poem also *becomes* a prayer for help in the midst of chaos and danger. The voice that speaks has survived a tsunami and appears to be in shock. Wearily she manages haltingly to say, "At least – to pray – is left – is left." The poignant repetition conveys her numb emotional state and implies that nothing much of her world remains. Both Earthquake and Maelstrom (lines 5–6) have brought about annihilation. The unusual word *maelstrom* is a favorite of Dickinson and appears in several poems. It refers to an exceptionally large or violent whirlpool (the Maelstrom is a marine whirlpool in northwestern Norway) and also to a situation marked by confusion, turbulence, violence, and heightened emotion. As one of my students used to say, "It's a splendid Wednesday word."

The survivor of this disaster turns to address Jesus in line 2. Instead of "Our Father who art in heaven," or "Papa above!" she cries, "Oh Jesus – in the Air." She is not sure where the Savior is, where his chamber, or room, is located. Being found "in the Air" is much less specific than either heaven or being "above." The one who prays flails about "knocking – everywhere." The action of knocking is significant, for it alludes to Matt 7:7: "Ask, and it shall be given you; seek, and ye shall find; knock, and it shall be opened unto you." Having sought and knocked everywhere, the poetic voice now pleads: you have set down the earthquake and the whirlpool, you have created the powers of the storm, don't you have a way to help me? Opening line 7 with the strongly stressed "Say," the poem asks for a comforting word, for God to speak. She's found the Savior's chambers at this point, identifying him as "Jesus Christ of Nazareth," just as Peter does in Acts 3 when he heals the lame man in the temple by invocation of that name. This formulaic appeal to God's authority is further indicated by the request for the "arm" of God, which throughout the King James translation refers to the power of God.

A stormy, tempestuous sea and a desperate cry for help—Peter also was once in these circumstances. After he bravely left his boat to walk on water toward Jesus in response to Christ's call, in the story told in Matthew 14, Peter's faith faltered when he encountered the boisterous wind. Sinking into the sea, he cried for help, and Jesus stretched forth his hand and caught him. He was saved by the arm of the Lord. In the occasional maelstroms of our lives, we can say with the poet, "At least – to pray – is left – is left." Along with Anne Lamott, my favorite prayer is, "help me, help me, help me!"

Devotion 9

Poem 411F (528J)

Mine – by the Right of the White Election!
Mine – by the Royal Seal!
Mine – by the sign in the Scarlet Prison –
Bars – cannot conceal!

Mine – here – in Vision – and in Veto!
Mine – by the Grave's Repeal –
Titled – Confirmed –
Delirious Charter!
Mine – long as Ages steal!

Consider: How do the legal words and images in the poem function? What do they represent or suggest to you?

An almost feverish celebration of faith, Poem 411 lays no uncertain claim to the promise of salvation articulated in the Scriptures—it's mine, mine, mine! This is a poem to chant aloud in a litany of assurance. That confidence is conveyed through structure, sound, and imagery. Dickinson rarely uses *anaphora*—the repetition of the same word or words at the beginning of two or more lines—but that technique, a basic tool in the Hebrew poetry of the Psalms, dominates this poem (although see Poem 114 for another use of anaphora). The sounds of the poem are similarly insistent in the strong stress of the trochee that opens each line but the eighth. And the dominant image pattern comes from legal philosophy, emphasizing "the Right" of the speaker to the promised assurance, with grand words such as *Election, Royal Seal, Veto, Repeal, Titled,* and *Charter.*

The legal language, however, is also theological language that anyone from a Calvinist tradition would quickly recognize. The elect, in Puritan thought, were those whom God has graciously chosen to receive salvation. The King James translation uses such language to speak of the saved: "Elect according to the foreknowledge of God the Father, through sanctification of the Spirit, unto obedience and sprinkling of the blood of Jesus Christ" (1 Pet 1:2). The "White Election" contrasts with the "Scarlet Prison," and echoes Isa 1:18: "Though your sins be as scarlet, they shall be as white as snow; though they be red as crimson, they shall be as wool." Election, salvation, and freedom are white; the prison of sin is scarlet.

The poem creates a mini drama somewhat reminiscent of the adventures of Paul and Silas in Philippi. We might think of it as a dramatic monologue in which the speaker has been imprisoned, shut up behind bars, and condemned to death, but at the last minute a royal reprieve arrives in the form of the King's own seal, a sign that cannot be denied or concealed. "Mine – by the Royal Seal!" the poet/prisoner exults, "Mine – by the sign in the Scarlet Prison - / Bars – cannot conceal!" The "Vision" and the "Veto," linked by alliteration, point to the effects of the royal pardon: a vision of life and a veto of death, repeated in "the Grave's Repeal." The speaker not only has been given a pardon, but she also has been granted a title. From condemned felon to a lady of the realm—the change is overwhelming, a "Delirious Charter!" And this is no ordinary elevation, for her new noble state will last for eternity, as "long as Ages steal!"

Much of the legal/theological imagery of this poem comes from Dickinson's beloved book of The Revelation of St. John the Divine. In chapter 7, John sees four angels standing on the four corners of the earth, preparing to destroy the world and everything within it. John describes, "And I saw another angel ascending from the east, having the seal of the living God: and he cried with a loud voice to the four angels, to whom it was given to hurt the earth and the sea, saying, Hurt not the earth, neither the sea, nor the trees, till we have sealed the servants of our God in their foreheads" (Rev 7:2–3). Thousands receive this seal and then join a great multitude dressed in white robes singing praises before the throne of the Lamb. The chapter ends with a stunning explanation of the new life in the heavenly court: "They shall hunger no more, neither thirst any more;

neither shall the sun light on them, nor any heat. For the Lamb which is in the midst of the throne shall feed them, and shall lead them unto living fountains of waters: and God shall wipe away all tears from their eyes" (Rev 7:16–17).

Dwelling in the house of the Lord as "long as Ages steal" sounds mighty fine to me, especially when I'm crying.

Devotion 10

Poem 429F (420J)

You'll know it – as you know 'tis Noon –
By Glory –
As you do the Sun –
By Glory –
As you will in Heaven –
Know God the Father – and the Son.

By intuition, Mightiest Things
Assert themselves – and not by terms –
"I'm Midnight" – need the Midnight say –
"I'm Sunrise" – Need the Majesty?

Omnipotence – had not a Tongue –
His lisp – is Lightning – and the Sun –
His Conversation – with the Sea –
"How shall you know"?
Consult your Eye!

Consider: What kinds of things do you know intuitively that you can't express adequately in language?

Naming things with a precise term is a poetic gift, one with which Emily Dickinson was amply blessed, but sometimes words and language are inadequate. Paradoxically, Poem 429 uses words to demonstrate both a serene confidence in God as well as the limits of language for speaking about God. The theme of this poem is what it means to "know," a word that appears four times. The poem speaks of knowing "By Glory," "By intuition," "by terms," and by "Consult[ing] your Eye" and explores how these different ways of knowing are related.

There is an implied question hanging in the air as the poem opens: how will I know it? Ironically, as readers we don't know what the "it" is, but the unnamed subject is presented in a series of three analogies: "you'll know it – as . . . ." First we are told that we will "know it" in a way similar to our knowledge of Noon and the Sun—"By Glory." By twice giving this brief one-stress phrase its own poetic line, the poet doubly emphasizes its importance. It almost sounds like a mild swear phrase, like "by gum." The word *glory* is an amazingly illusive and allusive term with many meanings, including majesty and splendor, beauty that inspires feelings of wonder or joy, and the idealized beauty and bliss of heaven. *Glory* denotes something that cannot be seen—a feeling, emotion, or intuition—so although we are able to recognize noon and the sun visually (the time at which the sun is located directly overhead; the brilliant orb that moves across the sky), strictly speaking neither can be perceived, for to gaze directly upon them would result in blindness. In the third analogy, we will know "it" in the same way that in heaven we will "Know God the Father – and the Son." The parallel of line 6 with lines 2 and 4 suggests that this is another way of saying "glory," adding another layer of meaning onto how we know. Our final heavenly "knowing" of God the Father and the Son will go beyond physically perceiving and emotionally experiencing to include firmly believing in and intimately associating with.

In the second stanza, knowing "by intuition" is contrasted with knowing "by terms," and the poet asserts that the "Mightiest Things" are known in the former manner, not necessarily through language. This claim resembles the controversial ideas of Horace Bushnell, a prominent nineteenth-century theologian who wrote, "Language has a literal character in regard to physical objects. . . . But, when we come to religion . . . our terms are only analogies, signs, shadows, so to speak, of the formless mysteries above us and within us."[1] In the posited dialogue, the poet seems to mock the idea that Midnight and the Sunrise would need to speak physically in order to identify themselves. "Terms," or words, throughout this poem

---

1. Noll, *America's God*, 294.

are associated with speech, as is indicated by the quotation marks of lines 9 and 10 and the references to "a Tongue," "lisp," and "Conversation." But instead of sound, "Omnipotence" asserts itself through sight—Lightning, the Sun, and the Sea. Psalm 19 plays with this same paradox of speaking about God's glory without language: "The heavens declare the glory of God; and the firmament sheweth his handwork. Day unto day uttereth speech, and night unto night sheweth knowledge. There is no speech nor language, where their voice is not heard."

The poem's overriding question is plainly stated in the penultimate line, with a succinct answer in the final line that packs into three words all the previous paradoxes and ambiguities: "'How shall you know'? / Consult your Eye!" This Eye is not only the physical eye of sensory experience, but also the inner eye (I) of intuition. In nineteenth-century America, intuition was commonly considered as one of the highest forms of knowing, both by liberal transcendentalists, such as Emerson, and conservative Presbyterians, such as Charles Hodge. Intuition involved the evidence of both the senses and consciousness, both of which are deemed necessary in Dickinson's account for the apperception of glory. It is fitting that we must exercise our own intuition in thinking about this poem, for although scholars have proposed several readings, the "it" to be recognized remains unnamed in the poem, left to intuition rather than terms.

Devotion 11

Poem 520F (442J)

God made a little Gentian –
It tried – to be a Rose –
And failed – and all the Summer laughed –
But just before the Snows   ·

There rose a Purple Creature –
That ravished all the Hill –
And Summer hid her Forehead –
And Mockery – was still –

The Frosts were her condition –
The Tyrian would not come
Until the North – invoke it –
Creator – Shall I – bloom?

Consider: What would you mean if you asked God, "Shall I bloom?"

The parable embodied in this narrative poem speaks to the reality of the fact that we all, at times, try to be something we are not. The year I turned thirty, like many women, I began to take stock and wonder whether my nonstop path through graduate school and into an academic career had been the right choice. Would it have been better to take time off and have had children? That very week, a friend of mine in her fifties, a professional woman with four wonderful children in their twenties, said to me,

"I remember turning 30; I was so depressed. I was stuck at home with four small children, and I thought that I would never have an adult conversation again with anyone besides my husband." We each were questioning the paths that we had taken.

Dickinson uses one of her favorite flowers, the fringed gentian, in her tale. She was an avid collector of flowers, roaming the fields and woods to find unusual species for her herbarium, a book of pressed flowers. A large leather volume with an embossed floral cover and a dark green spine, Dickinson's herbarium is now housed in the Houghton Library at Harvard University. It contains sixty-six pages with over four hundred specimens of both cultivated and wild flowers, each neatly labeled with its scientific name written in ink on a narrow strip of paper. Page 21 of Dickinson's herbarium contains a fringed gentian, a wildflower with trumpet-shaped flowers, which was only occasionally found near Amherst. Gentians can be blue, yellow, white, or red, but the one in this poem apparently is a purplish-blue (a color called *gentian blue*). "God made" this Gentian, which indicates its value, even if we didn't know that Dickinson was particularly fond of this rare wildflower. But the Gentian undertakes to be Rose and fails. Perhaps she sees a Rose as being more elegant, beautiful, or sophisticated. The little gentian's pretensions are the source of much merriment in the garden, as "all the Summer laughed" at her futile attempt.

In the next stage of the story, "just before the Snows" in the fall, when the early-blooming roses are all spent, "There rose a Purple Creature - / That ravished all the Hill." The Gentian blooms, and its sophisticated beauty is indicated with diction of *Creature* and *ravished*. Later in the poem, by being called "The Tyrian," the one from Tyre, and described as purple, the Gentian appears ancient and exotic. Surely the use of the word *rose* to indicate *grew* or *flowered* is not accidental, either. The scornful Miss Summer is now the ashamed party, hiding her face, as she ebbs away into fall, and "Mockery – was still." The beauty of the Gentian silences all criticism.

The final stanza explains the botanical reason for the late blooming of the Gentian: "The Frosts were her condition." It had to grow cold ("the North") first. The gentian blooms in the fall. "To every thing there is a season," and the gentian's season is fall (Eccl 3:1). The poet concludes the parable not by affixing a moral to the story; she is confident that we can grasp that for ourselves. Instead, the final line constitutes a prayer:

"Creator," she addresses the God who made both the Gentian and her, "Shall I – bloom?" Is her season come? Has she waited long enough, suffered through the necessary frost, to achieve a glorious beauty?

My friend, of course, at fifty was wise enough to see in retrospect that her despair at thirty was premature. Her season for professional achievement was yet to come. Her memories, however, allowed me to see that my season for being a mother had not yet come. When I am tempted to try to be something I am not—a creative cook, an expert seamstress, a person whose house is never a mess—I say to myself, "God made a little Gentian."

Devotion 12

Poem 581F (376J)

Of Course – I prayed –
And did God Care?
He cared as much as on the Air
A Bird – had stamped her foot –
And cried "Give Me" –
My Reason – Life –
I had not had – but for Yourself –
'Twere better Charity
To leave me in the Atom's Tomb –
Merry, and nought, and gay, and numb –
Than this smart Misery.

Consider: Have you ever prayed and not received an answer? How did you feel?

Many of the biblical Psalms are loud lamentations about God's failures: "Why art thou so far from helping me, and from the words of my roaring?" David complains in Psalm 22, "O my God, I cry in the daytime, but thou hearest not; and in the night season, and am not silent." Poem 581 reminds us of such psalms of pain, which may portray how we feel about God in those times in which it is difficult to hear God's voice, see God's hand, or feel God's presence.

The poem begins with a tart retort to some well-meaning but clueless friend who has recommended prayer as a balm for pain. "Of Course – I prayed," the poet bluntly replies in a line consisting solely of four strong stresses, with no weak beats mitigating its sharpness. Her bitterness is joined by sarcasm in the rhetorical question: "And did God Care?" As with most rhetorical questions, this is not a genuine inquiry, for the speaker merely wants to set us up for her answer, again sarcastically delivered: "He cared as much as on the Air / A Bird – had stamped her foot- / And cried 'Give Me.'" This bird sounds like a spoiled two-year-old with her mother at the grocery store, jumping up and down and whining, "give me, give me" in front of the candy display. And stamping your foot on the air isn't a particularly effective protest, either. Thinking about these descriptions, we may find the object of the sarcasm gradually shifting away from God to the one who complains.

Lines 5–7 can be read in multiple ways, granted such latitude by the ambiguous syntax and punctuation. Is the voice asking for a "Reason"? Explain to me why this has happened! Or, give me a tranquil mental state in the midst of such disturbed emotions that I fear I am going crazy! But if we assume more of a full stop, or period, after "Give Me," we hear the poet attempt to justify her desperate demands by providing the "Reason" for her prayer: I am requesting this help from you, God, because you gave me life; I wouldn't be alive if it wasn't for you. Working through these options, we find that the pivotal phrase is "My Reason," which occurs smack-dab in the middle of this eleven-line poem, so different in its format from Dickinson's typical four-line units. The fracture in logical language reveals how much is at stake here, as when David laments, "My heart is sore pained within me: and the terrors of death are fallen upon me. Fearfulness and trembling are come upon me, and horror hath overwhelmed me" (Ps 55:5–6).

At any rate, the final four lines comprise a coherent thought and further grievance against God. Why did you let me be born? It would have been a better demonstration of divine love, or charity, if I had been left "in the Atom's Tomb." Here the poem introduces an ingenious pun, drawing on both scientific and theological language. In nineteenth-century scientific thought, an atom referred to the smallest ultimate particle of matter, and combinations of atoms made up all physical bodies. In more common nineteenth-century usage, an atom was a mote of dust visible in a ray of sunlight. As a pun, however, the phrase refers to "Adam's Tomb," the rib of Adam out of which Eve was formed. The two associations come together in the fact that human life often is associated with dust in the

Bible, beginning with Adam's creation "of the dust of the ground" (Gen 2:7).

Existence before creation, before life, is described with a series of contrasts: "Merry, and nought, and gay, and numb." While we would probably prefer to be merry and gay, this pre-existent state is also described as being "nought," or nothing, and the final adjective, "numb" (connected to "nought" through alliteration), doesn't seem to permit much joy and happiness. The comparison signaled by "better" is completed in the final line's summing up of the poet's current state as "this smart Misery." The miserable state that has prompted the prayer "smarts," or hurts, but it also involves knowledge. Dickinson thus transforms the cliché "Ignorance is bliss." That may be so, but it is also "nought" and "numb"—neither of which are desirable or life affirming. (An archaic meaning of *nought* is wicked, connected to our word *naughty*.)

I keep going back to the wildly stamping Bird, though, which reminds us that God *does* care. "Are not two sparrows sold for a farthing?" Matthew records Jesus saying, "and one of them shall not fall on the ground without your Father. But the very hairs of your head are all numbered" (10:29–30). If such small, dumb, and insignificant creatures are looked after by God, wouldn't God also watch over me in the stinging pain prompted by consciousness? And while crying "Give me" seems whiney, it is also the request that Jesus teaches us to make in the Lord's Prayer: "Give us this day our daily bread." While David often concludes his psalms of lamentation, as in Psalms 22 and 55, by remembering God's saving grace, this poem offers only the oblique consolation that "smart Misery" is better than nothingness.

Devotion 13

Poem 613F (356J)

The Day that I was crowned
Was like the other Days –
Until the Coronation came –
And then – 'twas Otherwise –

As Carbon in the Coal
And Carbon in the Gem
Are One – and yet the former
Were dull for Diadem –

I rose, and all was plain –
But when the Day declined
Myself and It, in Majesty
Were equally – adorned –

The Grace that I – was chose –
To me – surpassed the Crown
That was the Witness for the Grace –
'Twas even that 'twas Mine –

Consider: How would you describe the tone of this poem? Exulting? Quiet?
Frantic? Proud? When have you felt this way?

When I was growing up in the early 60s, a popular daytime television program was called *Queen for a Day*. I don't remember the exact details of how the queen was selected, but each episode concluded with an ordinary housewife named "Queen for the Day," clad in an ermine fringed robe, handed an orb and scepter, and crowned with a sparkling diadem. She also won some appliance—a new fridge or washer/dryer combination—but I wasn't interested in that part. It was the crown that I found mesmerizing as a six-year-old.

In Poem 613 Dickinson's poetic persona calmly tells us about the day that she was crowned. Reading this poem against the Book of Revelation, we can imagine that this is the day that she receives "the crown of life" (Rev 2:10). The day starts out "like the other Days," no different from any that have gone before. She is not expecting that the day will be special or that she is going to receive this crown. But then "the Coronation came," and the day became radically different—"Otherwise." The first two lines are in iambic trimeter, but the third line has an extra beat, making it distinct. The alliteration of "Coronation came" looks back to "crowned" (line 1) and forward to the "Carbon" of the second stanza and the "Crown" of the final stanza.

Dickinson draws on her knowledge of chemistry, which she studied at Mount Holyoke, to develop an apt analogy in the second stanza. Coronation Day is to other days, as diamonds are to coal. Both diamonds and coal consist of the same chemical element, carbon, but they are strikingly different in appearance and use. Using coal would be "dull for Diadem," The third line of this quatrain is bumpy, metrically speaking, with three strong stresses and an extra weak beat. It's not as polished as the rest.

We return to the more straightforward discussion of the day in the third stanza, which focuses again on the unexpected change, the difference both in the day and in the self prompted by the coronation. In the morning, "I rose, and all was plain," both poet and day. The evening is then described with the wonderful phrase, "Day declined," which in its meaning of "sloping downward" reverses the action of the "I rose" in line 9, and alliteratively and imagistically resonates with the dull diadem of dark coal in the previous stanza. By nightfall, both self and day are identically clothed "in Majesty." They have become regal and dignified Queens.

The final stanza overtly states what the poem has implied all along: what most impresses the poet is not the glittering crown but the surprising fact that she was selected, "The Grace that I – was chose." The dash causes us to pause and ponder the "I" who has been "chosen . . . in him before the foundation of the world, [to] be holy and without blame before him in love" (Eph 1:4). It's the Grace that gets her, even though the Crown is "the Witness for the Grace," as the enjambment points out in another tetrameter line. The poem concludes with the poet almost shaking her head in disbelief, repeating again that the most amazing thing was "even that" grace was hers. (*Even* is used for emphasis to indicate something surprising, unlikely or extreme.) Concluding with the confident "Mine," the poem evokes the similar claim of "Mine – by the Right of the White Election." Grace has unbelievably been bestowed.

Devotion 14

Poem 632F (377J)

To lose One's faith – surpass
The loss of an Estate –
Because Estates can be
Replenished – faith cannot –

Inherited with Life –
Belief – but once – can be –
Annihilate a single clause –
And Being's – Beggary –

Consider: Have you ever lost your faith? Did you find it again?

The basic premise of this poem seems blatantly wrong. Faith can be re-plenished; I've witnessed it in my own life and in the lives of many others. Although not many people today are enamored of the Calvinist theol-ogy represented in the acronym TULIP,[1] the Perseverance of the Saints represented by the final letter has often been a great comfort to me. The Scriptures are full of stories of those whose faith has ebbed, like the dis-ciple Peter who betrays Christ three times, but eventually flows again. Many of us say daily with the tearful father of the disturbed son in Mark 9:24, "Lord, I believe; help thou mine unbelief." Yet this poem painfully

---

1. TULIP: Total Depravity, Unconditional Election, Limited Atonement, Irresistible Grace, and Perseverance of the Saints.

portrays the devastation of the loss of faith that may be felt in what John of the Cross called the dark night of the soul.

Filled with legal and economic diction, this poem relays the bitter cost of the loss of faith. That cost goes beyond losing "an Estate," that is, the whole of one's property, possessions, and capital. One who has been bankrupt may be able to restock or refill her estate through diligent hard work. But faith, the poem claims, cannot be "Replenished." An estate may also refer to the assets and liabilities left as an inheritance when some-one dies, and the second stanza picks up on this meaning. Like an estate, faith is "Inherited with Life." As Paul writes in Eph 2:10–11, "In Christ . . . we have obtained an inheritance." We are given new life when we have faith.

Line 6 repeats the faulty premise: "Belief – but once – can be." As we have seen, Dickinson herself held to "nimble believing," both believing and disbelieving a hundred times a day. But there are hours and days, and sometimes even weeks and months, in which our faith is so weak that when we consider our earlier unquestioning assurance, we feel that our faith is gone forever. At times like these we may say with this poem, "Belief – but once – can be." The legal language continues with the com-plete destruction of "a single clause," a section of a legal document that is usually separately numbered. The connotation of the term *annihilation* is violent and bleak, as is the result: "Being's – Beggary." Without belief, our existence becomes one of extreme poverty.

Yet is it true that the destruction of a single clause of our articles of faith is fatal? I know people who at one time strongly affirmed believer baptism who later in their lives embraced infant baptism. Surely the anni-hilating power depends on the centrality of the clause. Losing confidence that that God loves us, or that Jesus was the son of God, or that Christ rose from the dead would deal a more fatal blow.

The voice who speaks in this poem is too rigid, too simplistic. For her, life is black and white. You either believe, or you don't. You believe everything, or you believe nothing. Such absolutism leads to Beggary.

Devotion 15

Poem 724F (680J)

Each Life converges to some Centre –
Expressed – or still –
Exists in every Human Nature
A Goal –

Embodied scarcely to itself – it may be –
Too fair
For Credibility's presumption
To mar –

Adored with caution – as a Brittle Heaven –
To reach
Were hopeless, as the Rainbow's Raiment
To touch –

Yet persevered toward – surer – for the Distance –
How high –
Unto the Saints' slow diligence –
The Sky –

Ungained – it may be – by a Life's low Venture –
But then –
Eternity enable the endeavoring
Again.

Consider: What is the central goal of your life?

Because Dickinson sent a copy of the last stanza of this poem about vocation, the converging center of one's life, to her sister-in-law Sue with the signature, "Springfield," Dickinson's biographers have often assumed that the poem is about Samuel Bowles, a close friend and frequent visitor of the Dickinsons, dubbed "Uncle Sam" by Austin and Sue's children. Bowles was the hard-working editor of the influential *Springfield Republican*. He was a prolific writer, political activist, and advocate for women's rights, but also suffered from ill health and an unhappy marriage. His drive often outpaced his abilities, and he was plagued with a nagging sense of doubt about his life. Whether or not this poem describes Bowles, it also proposes to address a truth about "every Human Nature," including our own.

"Each Life," the poem posits, "converges to some Centre," and the unusual shape of the stanzas with their abrupt fourth lines reflect the idea of convergence, with the first stanza appropriately narrowing down to "A Goal." Everything in life, all our actions and experiences, coheres around some central aim or commitment. That goal might be "Expressed – or still," articulated or held silently deep within the heart. It might be "Embodied scarcely to itself," hardly even recognized or acknowledged by the self. Such silences exist because the goal is "too fair / For Credibility's presumption /To mar." The overconfidence of one eager to believe might spoil or detract from the beauty of the goal. To believe in oneself might be presumptuous.

The great yet fragile nature of such a life goal is suggested by the comparison to a "Brittle Heaven" and the need to use caution, even in admiration. Such dreams can easily shatter. Similarly, the impossibility of achieving the goal is conveyed in the comparison of attempting to touch the insubstantial "Rainbow's Raiment." The positive connotations of *Adored, heaven, rainbow*, and *fair* all convey the worthy nature of the goal.

The fourth stanza introduces an action toward the goal; until this point it has existed, been embodied, and been adored, but we haven't been allow to mar, to reach, or to touch it. Now it is "persevered toward," surely but slowly because of the distance. Another comparison (and pun) is introduced with "the Saints' slow diligence." Through hard work (Dickinson offers the alternative word *industry* for *diligence* in her fascicle), the saints slowly make their way to heaven ("The Sky"), but *diligence* is also a literary term for a stagecoach, so the word-picture displays the saints in a slow-moving coach laboriously driving up to the heavens.

We might fail to achieve our sky-high goal if we are not willing to risk, if we take "Life's low venture." Is this how Dickinson felt about Samuel Bowles? Even so, all is not lost. "But then," the poet concludes, "Eternity enable the endeavoring / Again." The unusual vowel alliteration of *es* and *as* and the length of the penultimate line (with six strong beats) draws it out in time. We will be able to work toward our goal again in eternity. If one of my goals is to exercise Christian charity toward a certain person, even if I don't achieve this aim on earth, I will be able to work toward such perfect love in heaven. This may seem like a strange idea if we've thought about heaven as a place of perfection and stasis and sitting around on clouds with harps, but why wouldn't we keep growing and developing? Isn't that how God created us to be?

If "Each Life converges to some Centre," what is at the heart of my efforts? Do I aim as high as the heavens, fragile and distant as that goal might be? Do I persevere with diligence and endurance? Do "I press toward the mark for the prize of the high calling of God in Christ Jesus?" (Phil 3:14).

Devotion 16

Poem 727F (698J)

Life – is what we make it –
Death – We do not know –
Christ's acquaintance with Him
Justify Him – though –   ·

He – would trust no stranger –
Other – could betray –
Just His own endorsement –
That – sufficeth Me –

All the other Distance
He hath traversed first –
No new mile remaineth –
Far as Paradise –

His sure foot preceding –
Tender Pioneer –
Base must be the Coward
Dare not venture – now –

Consider: How might Jesus be a "Tender Pioneer"? In what ways is he tender? What kind of new territory does he explore or open up?

Despite its deceptive opening line about life, this poem explores our common fear of death and provides solace for the unknown journey that we will all take, what Dickinson calls in another poem, "the Riddle, at the last." The contrast between life and death established in the first two lines is one of control and ignorance. The quality of our life, the poem implies, is something that we control. I'm not convinced that this is entirely accurate, but the second line rings true: "Death – We do not know." Perhaps compared to the mystery of death, we *are* able to make something of life.

Our comfort lies in the fact that Christ has an "acquaintance" with death, or as Isaiah puts it, "He is despised and rejected of men; a man of sorrows, and acquainted with grief" (53:3). That is what "Justify Him." The pronouns are flying fast and furious here, but I take the "Him" of both the third and fourth lines as referring to Death. There's almost a nineteenth-century social scene personified: we don't know Death, and he comes calling without an introduction, but then we learn that he knows our friend Christ, so that makes his apparently rude behavior acceptable. But we may also wonder about the theological connotations of "justify," being freed from sin through grace. How can Death be justified?

The pronoun reference shifts in the second stanza to refer to Christ again. The society-lady voice is speaking; Jesus wouldn't trust someone who was a stranger or who might be dangerous, so this unknown guest must be suitable. Christ's "endorsement" or public support is sufficient, good enough to satisfy us. But Dickinson doesn't write "satisfy," she uses "sufficeth," an old English word that goes back to the fourteenth century but, despite what we might expect, appears only once in the King James Bible, in John 14:8. The word *just* echoes the earlier *justify*, all of which suggests that this endorsement on the spiritual level is Christ's saving grace that justifies us and will take us through death to eternal life.

The motif of death as a long journey appears in the third stanza, with words such as *Distance, traversed, mile,* and *Far.* Christ has taken this journey before us, "no new mile remaineth," for he has gone through death all the way to "Paradise." Christ is thus our "Tender Pioneer"; like the intrepid Americans travelling to and settling in Michigan, Illinois, and Missouri during Dickinson's time, Christ has gone with sure feet into previously uncharted territory and conquered it. That's why he can justify death. We tend to think of pioneers as tough and hardy stock, but Christ is tender, loving and caring, described as a "tender plant" in Isa 53:2 and full "of tender mercy" in Jas 5:11.

Given such a pioneer breaking ground before us and encouraging us in our journey, we would be low and cowardly if we "Dare not venture

– now." The implication of *adventure* fits with the pioneering story, but a *venture* also refers to an undertaking that involves risk but could lead to profit. It will take courage to go through death, but Christ will be our surefooted guide.

Devotion 17

Poem 800F (1052J)

I never saw a Moor.
I never saw the Sea –
Yet know I how the Heather looks
And what a Billow be –

I never spoke with God
Nor visited in Heaven –
Yet certain am I of the spot
As if the Checks were given –

Consider: What's the connection between the claims of the first stanza and the claims of the second stanza?

A simple affirmation of faith drawn by means of an analogy, this poem subtly reminds us of the imaginative power of a text to speak truth. The simple repetition and straightforward syntax of the first two lines admit ignorance: the poet has never seen, or witnessed first-hand, either a "Moor" or "the Sea." Our confusion as to which kind of "Moor" she is referring (the Shakespearean character of Othello, perhaps?) is soon resolved with the reversals of the next two lines. Despite not having seen a Moor, she does know "how the Heather looks"; despite not having encountered the sea, she can define "what a Billow be." These two geographical phenomenon are not present in the Connecticut River Valley where Dickinson spent most of her life, but she would have known about them through books. In the same way, I've never been to the fabled Cambodian city of Angkor Wat or the ashy ruins of Pompeii, yet I know about soaring Hindu temples and the preserved bodies of chained Roman gladiators.

The heather-covered moor and the stormy weather producing billows rather than waves bring to mind Emily Bronte's dark romance *Wuthering Heights*, which Dickinson had appreciatively read. She felt a deep affinity with both Emily Bronte and her sister Charlotte. Dickinson's favorite poem was Emily Bronte's "Last Lines," which Thomas Wentworth Higginson read at her funeral, by her request. Like Emily Dickinson, Emily Bronte possessed the powerful ability to use language to bring Heather to life.

The second stanza of this poem follows a pattern similar to the first stanza: two lines reflect on an absence or lack of experience, followed by a turn in meaning signaled by the mighty little word "Yet." Only now we are in the realm of religious experience, described in language that evokes a social relationship. "I never spoke with God," the poet admits, "Nor visited in Heaven." I'm struck by the way the word *prayer* isn't used in the first line, just as the second doesn't talk about dying. Rather, the impression we get is of someone who has withdrawn from the social scene—isn't talking to or visiting with others, like Dickinson in her later years. In a literal sense, none of us have ever "spoke with God" by carrying on a conversation, even if we have prayed; nor have we spent a day visiting "in heaven." At times of doubt, we long for such concrete encounters—to be able to call God up on the telephone or to drop in at the New Jerusalem for afternoon tea.

"Yet"—the third line calls to us to leave such doubt behind—"certain am I of the spot." The non-poets among us, among whom I include myself, probably would have written "Yet I am certain of the spot," but the line's more awkward wording emphasizes the assurance by putting the first strong stress of the line on cér-tain: Yĕt cértaĭn ăm Ĭ ŏf thĕ spót. The conviction is so strong that it is "As if the Checks were given." The image of a check suggests several possibilities. It could refer to a written order directing a banker to pay a sum of money, or to a mark made against an item in an account, but, given the railroading mania of the nineteenth-century, I think "the Checks" refers to the tokens given at a railway station or cloakroom to someone who turns in luggage that will be reclaimed later. According to the *Oxford English Dictionary*, this is a particularly American usage of "check," one which first gained currency in the nineteenth century. (Dickinson's early editors were so flummoxed by the ambiguity of *Checks*, however, that they regularly changed the word to *chart*, as if the speaker could consult a map to locate God and heaven.)

The poet is so certain of the existence of God's heaven that she feels as if she is holding a token in her hand that indicates she has checked her luggage through to the final destination. It's as if the reality of a long-awaited dream vacation sinks in only when you hold the baggage claim slip in your hand at the airport. And since the affirmation of moors and seas came from reading, perhaps our assurance of "the spot" also comes from a text—the Bible. The scene described in Revelation may serve as our "check"—our verification—of a reality that we have not yet witnessed personally but often long to enter.

Devotion 18

Poem 825F (964J)

"Unto Me"? I do not know you –
Where may be your House?

"I am Jesus – Late of Judea –
Now – of Paradise" –

Wagons – have you – to convey me?
This is far from Thence –

"Arms of Mine – sufficient Phaeton –
Trust Omnipotence" –

I am spotted – "I am Pardon" –
I am small – "The Least
Is esteemed in Heaven the Chiefest –
Occupy my House" –

Consider: Who is talking in this poem? What is the topic of their conversation?

A tender dialogue between the poetic voice and Jesus, this poem portrays in simple and poignant language the call to salvation in the most orthodox of terms. Jesus' voice appears within quotation marks, welcoming, explaining, reassuring. The initially ignorant and then insecure poetic persona offers numerous objections, but Jesus has answers for every doubt, and the poem gives him the final word.

We begin to listen in the middle of the conversation. Jesus has just issued a compelling invitation, "Come unto me, all ye that labour and are heavy laden, and I will give you rest. Take my yoke upon you, and learn of me; for I am meek and lowly in heart: and ye shall find rest unto your souls" (Matt 12:28–29). The poet responds by quoting two words of the invitation in puzzlement, wondering about the identity of the person who makes such promises. "I do not know you," she says. "Where may be your House?" It's almost as if a stranger has stopped her in the street and invited her to visit. Jesus responds by giving his name and his residence, even colloquially indicating that he has recently had a change of address: "Late of Judea - / Now – of Paradise." Well, that's a long way to travel to visit you, the poet responds, "Wagons – have you – to convey me?" How can I possibly get there?

Despite receiving an extremely hospitable invitation, our speaker offers several objections. First she wants to know who this person is, then she wonders where he lives, and finally she says that his house is too far away. But Jesus offers transportation: "Arms of Mine – sufficient Phaeton." A light four-wheeled carriage, a phaeton was usually drawn by two horses, and Jesus' arms will serve as that carriage. As Isaiah says, "He shall feed his flock like a shepherd: he shall gather the lambs with his arm, and carry them in his bosom" (40:11). Perhaps tiring of all these objections, Jesus adds, "Trust Omnipotence," the unlimited power, authority, and knowledge of God.

But the introduction of such grandeur prompts further doubts, and the exchanges between the two speakers become even more rapid, indicating Christ's ready answers to all objections. "I am spotted," the poet admits, a sinful creature. "I am Pardon," Christ responds. But I am small and insignificant, says the poet, why would you want me to visit your house? The disciples had similar objections when little children were brought to Jesus for prayer and a blessing, but Jesus rebuked them, advising "for of such is the kingdom of heaven" (Matt 19:14). "The Least / Is esteemed in Heaven the Chiefest," the poem's Jesus says, paraphrasing Matt 19:20: "But many that are first shall be last; and the last shall be first." In heaven, even those who are small and have many questions will be valued highly.

The poem concludes with a final invitation, similar to the one implied in the opening two words, but issued a bit more tersely, "Occupy my

House." In Dickinson's manuscript, she has indicated an alternative final line of "Occupy my Breast," which seems more lovingly personal, but the image of the House effectively circles to the beginning of the poem and the question concerning the location of the house in line 2.

In no other poem does Dickinson, or her "supposed speaker," confess that she is a sinner when confronted with God's power and authority. The skeptical may note that the poetic dialogue does not contain a resolution; we don't know whether the speaker accepts Jesus' invitation, leaps in his arms, and journeys to Paradise, but we hope that she does.

Devotion 19

Poem 911F (951J)

As Frost is best conceived
By force of it's Result –
Affliction is inferred
By subsequent effect –

If when the Sun reveal,
The Garden keep the Gash –
If as the Days resume
The wilted countenance

Cannot correct the crease
Or counteract the stain –
Presumption is Vitality
Was somewhere put in twain –

Consider: Have you ever experienced something that you might call "afflic-tion"? When? How did this experience affect you?

In this poem, Dickinson establishes a controlling analogy—frost is like affliction—in the first stanza and then devotes the next two stanzas to describing the effects of frost, leaving us to draw out the analogy's impli-cations for affliction ourselves. For someone like myself who grew up liv-ing at an azalea nursery, or farm, this application is not too difficult. Each summer, my family's annual crop of azaleas was transplanted from our greenhouses to outdoor beds where they enjoyed the Pacific Northwest air until fall, when they were either shipped off to our customers or moved back into their heated glass houses. One early September frost, and a whole year's income was lost. For my family, frost *was* affliction.

As gardeners know, frost is a tricky character. Dickinson advises that it is best understood "by force of it's [sic] Result." That is, do the plants die? How strong or severe has the frost been? Was it mild or deep? Did it last a few minutes or several hours? Affliction functions similarly; it isn't always readily apparent. Instead it must be "inferred / By subsequent effect." Inferences are conclusions that an observer draws based on evidence or reasoning. We, those outside affliction, the ones not experiencing it, must deduce its existence by virtue of its effects.

The extent of damage caused by a frost takes some time to observe. In the early morning after a hard freeze, our flowers might not look all that different. But frostbit plants, like frostbit fingers, will gradually wither, turn black, and die. Some, more lightly touched then others, might have their tender buds destroyed but maintain their foliage. And others may look slightly wilted for a few days but then bounce back to full health. So we must wait for "the Sun [to] reveal" and "the Days resume." By personifying the garden flowers as having a "countenance," or face, that has become creased, or wrinkled, the poet subtly keeps the human half of the analogy before us. If the flowers "Cannot correct the crease / Or counteract the stain" after a few days, we know that the frost has damaged them.

The laconic closing lines of the poem point again to the mental work of the observer: our "Presumption is Vitality / Was somewhere put in twain." We presume or deduce what has happened; the life force of the plant (its vitality) has been severed, cut in two. The cutting imagery refers back to "the Gash" in the Garden, which alliteratively emphasizes the violence of the destruction.

When our friends or family experience the blow of a killing frost, the effects may not be immediately noticeable. The affliction they have sustained may only gradually emerge. If we are to provide loving support, we must observe, and infer, and presume, to see how deep the Gash goes.

Devotion 20

Poem 978F (915J)

Faith – is the Pierless Bridge
Supporting what We see
Unto the Scene that We do not –
Too slender for the eye

It bears the Soul as bold
As it were rocked in Steel
With Arms of steel at either side –
It joins – behind the Vail

To what, could We presume
The Bridge would cease to be
To Our far, vascillating Feet
A first Nescessity.

Consider: What ideas concerning faith does this poem suggest for you?

A definition poem, a genre that Dickinson used occasionally, Poem 978 opens with the single word that is going to be explained: the one-syllable, strong-stressed topic of the poem: Faith. And as Dickinson loves to do, she then explores the meaning of faith with an elaborate metaphor, on which we must dwell in order to tease out all the complex meanings and implications.

Paradox and pun come together in the first line with the introduction of the controlling metaphor: "the Pierless Bridge." The piers of a bridge are the vertical structural supports between two spans, and without any piers, how could a bridge stand? Yet the pun also suggests that the bridge is "peerless," incomparable or without equal, very precious indeed. A suspension bridge could be described as being pierless, for its deck is suspended from cables moored in the ground at either end, rather than held up by a series of Roman style arches and piers. The first major American suspension bridge was built over the Niagara River below Niagara Falls in 1855; it was the only engineering technique capable of uniting the 821-foot gorge in a single span. It paved the way for its more famous cousin, the Brooklyn Bridge, constructed in 1883. (This poem was probably written about 1864 or 1865, so Dickinson might have had the Niagara Falls bridge in mind.)

So let's think about the Bridge of Faith as a suspension bridge, stretching between "what We see" on one end and, on the other, what we cannot see—described in another mischievous pun as "the Scene [seen] that We do not." The bridge itself cannot be made out either, as it is too "slender," or thin. As Heb 11:1 says, "Now faith is the substance of things hoped for, the evidence of things not seen." Yet the sentence begun in the fourth line runs without a dash or mark of punctuation into the second stanza to present a paradox of a slight bridge that nonetheless is as strong as "Steel," bearing the "Soul" boldly and confidently. The bridge is personified, almost as an attentive mother, with "Arms of steel" that carry the soul, rocking it gently for comfort. The "Arms of steel at either side" might be two primary cables suspending the pierless bridge.

In line 8 we return to the scene that we cannot see—the other side of the bridge, where stiffening trusses and cable stays tie the deck superstructure to the walls of the gorge. There is a "Vail" of fog or steam that obscures our vision of the place where the cables anchor the pierless bridge to the wall on the far side (*vail* occasionally was an alternative spelling for *veil* in the nineteenth century). We can easily envision such vapors obscuring our vision in the physical world; a renowned waterfall in Yosemite is charmingly called "Bridal Veil Falls." On the metaphoric level, though, the Vail alludes to the curtain in the Jewish temple that hid from ordinary eyes the Holy of Holies, containing the Ark of the Covenant and the Mercy Seat. Only the high priest was allowed to enter this most holy place, in order to plead for mercy. The temple veil was torn in two at the time of Christ's death (Matt 27:51), and the book of Hebrews associates our hope of salvation with the images of anchor, strength, and veil: "Which hope we have as an anchor of the soul, both sure and steadfast, and which entereth into that within the veil; Whither the forerunner is for us entered, even Jesus, made an high priest for ever after the order of Melchisedec" (Heb 6:19–20). "Going beyond the veil" was a common nineteenth-century euphemism for death, used especially by spiritualists and table rappers who attempted to contact the dead with séances and Ouija boards.

"To what" the bridge joins, we cannot see, and there is similarly no punctuation spanning the gap between the second and the third stanza. But if we could boldly assume what is on the other side of the veil, what mercy lies beyond death, we would not need faith; the bridge would not be "a first Nescessity" (Dickinson misspelled the word, along with *vascillating* in the previous line, inserting an extra *s* in both). This movement of our feet suggests an unsteady gait as well as wavering confidence, but how would we describe feet as "far"? If we think of the word in terms of the future, the last three lines point to a time yet to come, when our wavering feet will need the strong arms of faith to support us through the veil of death to the as yet unseen scene. The invisible Bridge of Faith may mysteriously float above the rapids and lead to the unknown, but it will carry us securely.

Devotion 21

Poem 1046F (1086J)

What Twigs We held by –
Oh the View
When Life's swift River striven through
We pause before a further plunge
To take Momentum –
As the Fringe
Opon a former Garment shows
The Garment Cast,
Our Props disclose
So scant, so eminently small
Of Might to help, so pitiful
To sink, if We had labored, fond
The diligence were not more blind

How scant, by everlasting Light
The Discs that satisfied our sight –
How dimmer than a Saturn's Bar
The Things esteemed, for Things that are!

Consider: What might be the difference between things that we esteem, or think highly of, and "things that are"?

A retrospective look at life often shows events in a different light. The voice speaking in this poem is mature, shaking her head and tisk-tisking over the follies of youth. "What Twigs We held by," she exclaims of her early years making her way through "Life's swift River." This initial image of ineffectually clutching a thin branch in the midst of dangerous rapids is the first of many diminutive terms in the poem, including *Fringe, scant, small, pitiful, blind,* and *dimmer.* The poetic speaker continues in the exclamatory mode to comment on the view that one has at the end of life, when one "pause[s] before a further plunge," gathering strength for the final effort, readying oneself to push off and gain "Momentum." The capital letter and Latinate term suggest that this is a weighty, or momentous moment.

Line 6 introduces a difficult analogy comparing "the Fringe" of a garment to "Our Props," those things that provide comfort or assistance. The garment is described as "former," because now, at the point of death, one is getting ready to put on a new garment of glory. Nineteenth-century dresses often were adorned with elaborate fringes, which would inform the observer about the kind, or style, or quality of the dress. Silk, velvet, and lace were all used to make fringes. When a woman was wearing black because she was in mourning, the first movement out of mourning might be to change the black fringe on her dress to a more subtle gray or lavender. In a similar way, "our Props disclose," or provide information.

I take the "Props" to be another way of referring to the "Twigs" of the opening line, and like the fragile twigs, they reveal a meager lack of substance. Dickinson employs an especially effective oxymoron in the description of the Props being "eminently small / Of Might to help." Their lack of assistance is so "pitiful," that we might "sink" while attempting to make our way through the swift river of life, laboring to survive. Our misconception of those things that might hold us up is indicated by the archaic meaning of *fond* as gullible or easily led to believe something that is not true. Our "diligence," or hard work, is "blind."

The syntactically dense and rhythmically rough first stanza is followed by a final stanza made up of two simple couplets that more clearly state the theme of the poem. Picking up on the imagery evoked by "blind," as well as repeating the "scant" found in line 10, the poet unfavorably compares "The Discs that satisfied our sight" on the earth to the "everlasting Light." What we once found startlingly brilliant now appears scant and dim, as barely perceptible as the rings of light surrounding the planet Saturn. Isaiah relates a similar change of perspective: "The sun shall be no more thy light by day; neither for brightness shall the moon give light unto thee: but the Lord shall be unto thee an everlasting light, and thy God thy glory. Thy sun shall no more go down; neither shall thy moon withdraw itself: for the Lord shall be thine everlasting light, and the days of thy mourning shall be ended" (Isa 60:19–20).

The contrast articulated in the final line of the poem is crucial: we tend to esteem or highly prize certain things in this life, but they are actually scant, dull, and ineffective. "Things that are" are more real, sufficient, brilliant, and eternal. What dim discs might I be currently depending on?

Devotion 22

Poem 1063F (871J)

The Sun and Moon must make their haste –
The Stars express around
For in the Zones of Paradise
The Lord alone is burned –

His Eye, it is the East and West –
The North and South when He
Do concentrate His Countenance
Like Glow Worms, flee away –

Oh Poor and Far –
Oh Hindered Eye
That hunted for the Day –
The Lord a Candle entertains
Entirely for Thee –

*Consider: What are the properties of a candle and what might it mean for
God to light a candle for you?*

The colossal and the small, the grandiose and the humble, the daunting
and the comforting—this poem runs the gamut of extremes in its exploration of the facets of God, who is referred to as "The Lord." The apocalyptic
feeling evoked by the poem comes primarily through the majestic images
of the first two stanzas, which are then starkly reversed in the simple com-

fort provided by the final stanza. It's as if we, like Elijah, have witnessed a tempestuous wind, mountain-shattering earthquake, and raging fire only to find God in a still small voice (1 Kgs 19:11–12).

The most dominant image of the poem is that of light. It opens with references to the three cosmic light bearers named in Gen 1:16—the Sun, Moon, and Stars. All three are compelled ("must") to move rapidly, to make haste, to "express around." What's the hurry? The opening word of line 3 informs us that the explanation is forthcoming: "For in the Zones of Paradise / The Lord alone is burned." We are moving into a different time zone, as it were, the zone of paradise, in which the only cosmic light bearer is the Lord. Very much like the passage in Isaiah that we noted in the previous meditation, Revelation describes the change in lighting this way: "The city had no need of the sun, neither of the moon, to shine in it: for the glory of God did lighten it, and the Lamb is the light thereof" (21:23). The temporal time zone is coming to an end, and the sun, moon, and stars seem to be rapidly traversing the sky as time itself speeds up, like a scene out of *2001: A Space Odyssey*. The solemnity of the moment is reinforced with a series of long *o* sounds: for, zones, lord, alone.

The magnificent cosmic picture continues in the second stanza with the naming of the four points of the compass. The Lord's Eye is now the East and West: the points from which the sun used to rise and set. The North and the South "flee away" from the brightness of his "Countenance," just as glowworms, or fireflies, disappear at the rising of the morning sun. (Notice the long *o* again in glowworm.) Both geography and time are no more as God's burning presence overwhelms the world. It is an eerie picture, almost threatening in its immensity and power.

In contrast, a person, perhaps us, appears—"Poor and Far." We have no resources, and we are distant; perhaps we, too, like the North and South have fled from the awesome face of God. Our Eye, in stark contrast to His omniscient Eye, is "Hindered," obstructed or unable to see. This eye has "hunted for the Day," but has been unable to find it, since sunrise and sunset have swiftly fled to leave "The Lord alone" to burn. The last stanza initially sounds like a lament, with the anaphoric "Oh" keening in sorrow, but it ultimately turns into an admonition to the poor, distant, blinded eye. Take comfort in the midst of the dissolution of time and space, the final stanza counsels, for "The Lord a Candle entertains / Entirely for Thee." Another echo from Revelation appears in this final image: "They need no candle, neither light of the sun; for the Lord God giveth them light"

(22:5). I find particular charm in the choice of the word *entertain*, with its connotation of offering domestic hospitality, while the concentrated personal attention of *Entirely* indicates that even in the midst of huge cosmic transformations, God will care for *me*.

The paradisiacal candle is, of course, the Lord himself, who is described as being "burned" in line 4. But this is an eternal flame that will never be diminished, continually offering joy, perception, hospitality, and comfort, entirely for me.

Devotion 23

Poem 1100F (1100J)

The last Night that She lived
It was a Common Night
Except the Dying – this to Us
Made Nature different

We noticed smallest things –
Things overlooked before
By this great light opon our minds
Italicized – as 'twere.

As We went out and in
Between Her final Room
And Rooms where Those to be alive
Tomorrow, were, a Blame

That others could exist
While She must finish quite
A Jealousy for Her arose
So nearly infinite –

We waited while She passed –
It was a narrow time –
Too jostled were Our Souls to speak
At length the notice came.

She mentioned, and forgot –
Then lightly as a Reed
Bent to the Water, struggled scarce –
Consented, and was dead –

And We – We placed the Hair –
And drew the Head erect –
And then an awful leisure was
Belief to regulate –

Consider: What emotions does the poem describe someone having while witnessing the death of another?

Emily Dickinson wrote many famous poems about death, such as "Because I could not stop for Death," "Death is the supple Suitor," and "I heard a Fly buzz – when I died," which use unusual, unexpected images to spotlight the process of human demise in a sudden and striking fashion. This poem about death is quite different: calm, measured, sturdy—it tells a straightforward narrative in relatively simple language. Yet its quiet language and tone, the "Common Night" (with its incongruous capital letters) it chronicles, capture both the ordinariness and the strangeness of death and its relationship to faith.

The prosaic language and syntax of the first two lines create an almost conversational effect: "The last Night that She lived / It was a Common night." But the run-on line introduces an anomaly in the phrase "Except the Dying." The use of the definite article *the* here is unusual, naming the event as generic or universal. And the choice of the gerund (*dying*, rather than *death*) points us to the extended process, rather than the finality of the event. What takes place this "last Night" makes "Nature different," causing "Us" to see the world around us in a new way. This poem is narrated in a communal voice; "the Dying" gives everyone a new way of seeing.

What once was small is now noticed, like the mundane insect in "I heard a Fly buzz." "Things overlooked before" become "italicized – as 'twere." We use italics to call attention to something—a proper name, a foreign word, an emphasis—and line 8 self-consciously points to the fact that the poet is employing a metaphor ("as 'twere"), in effect italicizing the imagery. These new perceptions are made possible by the "great light" of "the Dying." The second stanza closes with a rare (for Dickinson) use of a period, reinforcing the prosaic rhythm of the poem's opening. The ordinary has become extraordinary.

The next two stanzas are much more complex and syntactically ambiguous, alternating between two competing ideas in the same way that "We," the family and friends who are present, move between "Her final Room" and the other rooms of the house. The latter are named indirectly by contrast: "Rooms where Those to be alive / Tomorrow, were." The rest of the people in this poem will be alive tomorrow; the dying woman will not. The "Blame" that follows is grammatically ambiguous: should we be blamed for being alive tomorrow? Or does the enjambment carry us to the idea that it is unfortunate "That others could exist / While She must finish quite"? This second reading provokes even more uncertainties, for are we more misfortunate to exist or to finish? Just as "a Blame" could grammatically go with either the phrase before or after it, so the "quite" of line 14 could modify either "finish" or "A Jealousy," denoting either/ both "finish completely" or "a considerable degree of jealousy." While these stanzas clearly describe the physical movement of the people, their emotional fluctuations of Blame and Jealousy are erratic and unclear. Nonetheless, we can say that our envy of the dying woman comes from the fact that she is "so nearly infinite," so close to an existence without limits, so near heaven.

We have newly seen the previously overlooked; we have restlessly roamed through the rooms of the house; and now we wait while the woman dies, passing from one state of existence to another—the infinite. "It was a narrow time," cramped, restricted, hard to handle. "Our Souls" are "jostled," knocked about in the narrow confines of the time, and we cannot speak, but eventually we receive some kind of sign, or notice, that the end is near. Perhaps the doctor tells us that the woman only has a few more minutes; perhaps the sound of her breathing grows more labored.

The dying woman now speaks, but the poem does not tell us what she says: "She mentioned" someone or something, but she also "forgot." Then the moment of death occurs, described with a beautifully evocative simile taken from nature: "lightly as a Reed / Bent to the Water, struggled scarce – / Consented, and was dead." There is no struggle; the woman lightly bends and acquiesces, like a tall slender plant gently bowed by a stream of water.

We are left to cope with the physical and emotional aftermath. First we must tend to the corpse, as nineteenth-century women often did, arranging the dead woman's hair and placing her head neatly "erect" in the coffin after the reed-like bending of the previous stanza. Our emotional numbness is already indicated in the repetition of "And We – We" and the mechanical "And," "And," "And" of lines 25–27, but it is explicitly described in the "awful leisure" we now experience. Our work is done; we no longer can care for the sick woman, watch at her deathbed, or even prepare her body for burial. With nothing to do, we begin to feel, which makes this time of leisure horrifying. Only belief can "regulate," or control and organize, the extremity of our shock and sorrow. And that regulation may take some time; fortunately we have the leisure, awful though it may be.

Devotion 24

Poem 1102F (1097J)

Dew – is the Freshet in the Grass –
'Tis many a tiny Mill
Turns unperceived beneath – our feet
And Artisan lies still –

We spy the Forests and the Hills
The Tents to Nature's Show
Mistake the Outside for the in
And mention what we saw.

Could Commentators on the Sign
Of Nature's Caravan
Obtain "admission" as a Child
Some Wednesday Afternoon.

*Consider: What kind of scene is suggested with the words **tents, show, caravan, admission,** and **afternoon?** What kinds of feelings are evoked by this scene?*

Emily Dickinson loved "tiny" things, including bees, butterflies, children, poems, and daisies. She herself was frail, slender, and small of stature. In this poem, Dickinson asks us to pay attention to something in nature that we may have previously overlooked: dew. She unexpectedly describes this tiny natural phenomenon as "the Freshet in the Grass." Now the word *freshet* has a lovely clean watery sound, but it usually refers to a much larger body of water than drops of dew. A *freshet* is a flash flood: a sudden rise in the water level of a river caused by heavy precipitation or a sudden thaw, especially after a period of dry weather. Spring freshets were common after a snowy New England winter. After opening with the tiny Dew, then expanding to the large Freshet, the poem's first line returns us to the diminutive with its location of this flood "in the Grass." Where does this sudden though small influx of water come from? The rest of the first stanza alludes to a Lilliputian world of "a tiny [wind] Mill" turning underneath our feet, run by a quiet "Artisan," or skilled craftsperson, all "unperceived" by us.

We tend to pay more attention to larger natural phenomena—the towering forests and looming hills. But the poem insists that these are merely "The Tents to Nature's Show," the exterior housing the real action, the dazzlingly white big top containing the daring performers and exotic animals. We "Mistake" this external display "for the in," which results in a muted response—a "mention" rather than a proclamation, or celebration, or exultation.

The third stanza expands the circus metaphor first suggested by the image of the tents. A caravan is a covered vehicle used by circus performers as a traveling home, and the final two lines refer to paying a child's admission price, which was typically half price for those under twelve during Dickinson's time. Although circus performances in the United States originated in the colonial period, it wasn't until the 1830s that attending a circus became a common form of entertainment, and traveling circuses reached their peak of popularity following the Civil War. When a circus entered a small New England village, such as Amherst, it would parade through the streets in an attempt to drum up an audience before setting up its tents on the outskirts of town. We know from her letters that Emily liked to sit in her bedroom window and watch the spectacle of the circus marching into Amherst, but there is no evidence that she ever attended a performance.

Using the metaphor of the circus, the poet contrasts the "Commentators," who are limited to speaking about the signs festooning the sides of the caravans, advertising the amazing sights that can be seen within the big top, with "a Child," who obtains admission or is allowed in, and here we begin to find a subtle indication of another kind of meaning. The Child who is permitted to enter reminds us of the children that the disciples tried to keep from Jesus. "Suffer little children to come unto me," Jesus calls, "and forbid them not: for of such is the kingdom of God. Verily I say unto you, Whosoever shall not receive the kingdom of God as a little child shall in no wise enter therein" (Luke 18:16–17). A simple, childlike faith is what is required to enter the tents of heaven, not sophisticated theological commentary.

The opening conditional "Could" of the third stanza seem to suggest that the poet wishes that "Commentators on the Sign" would enter the tent, would see the real show. And this concept of what they *don't* see brings us back to the opening image of the dew. In the Bible, dew is often associated with God's providential care: Isaac blesses his son Jacob with these words: "God give thee of the dew of heaven, and the fatness of the earth, and plenty of corn and wine" (Gen 27:28). Similarly, the manna provided to the children of Israel in the wilderness appears when the morning dew dissipates (Exod 16:13–14). In one of those oblique thought-reverberations found so often in Emily Dickinson's poetry, dew is thus associated with a kind of bread or corn (ground up at a mill). But it also alludes to childhood, as in "the dew of thy youth" (Ps 110:3), and so we return full circle to the final stanza.

When we notice and comment on the grandiose but distant elements of nature, rather than the miraculous operation of the nearby dew, we are like a New England villager who idly speculates about the circus without having ever seen its wonders. But we are also like arrogant apostles or biblical commentators who "Mistake the Outside for the in" and merely "mention" what we see rather than lifting the tent flap and entering into the circus-like joy of the kingdom.

Devotion 25

Poem 1261F (1241J)

The Lilac is an ancient Shrub
But ancienter than that
The Firmamental Lilac
Opon the Hill Tonight –
The Sun subsiding on his Course
Bequeathes this final plant
To Contemplation – not to Touch –
The Flower of Occident.

Of one Corolla is the West –
The Calyx is the Earth –
The Capsule's burnished Seeds the Stars –
The Scientist of Faith
His research has but just begun –
Above his Synthesis
The Flora unimpeachable
To Time's Analysis –
"Eye hath not seen" may possibly
Be current with the Blind
But let not Revelation
By Theses be detained –

Consider: What do you think a "Scientist of Faith" is? Are you one? Was Dickinson?

Like many of us, Emily Dickinson loved sunsets, "the Firmamental Lilac." I live a few blocks away from Sunset Park, a narrow strip of grass and flowers perched on a hill above Puget Sound looking out toward the Olympic Mountains in the west. When the sun sets, especially during the summer, the park is full of neighbors who silently watch as the huge glowing orb steadily slips behind the mountains or sinks into the sea (depending on the sun's position in the horizon). While the Psalms are full of appreciation for the presence of God in huge thunderstorms, I find sunsets one of the places where I am especially attuned to the goodness of God's creation.

This poem has a deceptive opening, initially appearing to be another one of Dickinson's flower poems. The syntactically simple first line is straightforward and blunt. The first thing about a lilac that comes to my mind is its sweet fragrance, but the poet singles out its age; it is "an ancient Shrub." Dickinson's garden at the Homestead had several lilac bushes, and their ancient quality is evidenced in the fact that some of these shrubs still bloom today, as you can see (and smell) if you visit Amherst in May. The "turn" that appears in so many of Dickinson's poems shows up already in the second line of what, for Dickinson, is a long poem: "But ancienter than that / The Firmamental Lilac." *Firmament* is a grand-old, King-James-Bible, literary word for sky that permeates the Genesis 1 creation story. "In the beginning God created the heaven and the earth" and separated light from darkness. "And God called the light Day, and the darkness he called Night. And the evening and the morning were the first day. And God said, Let there be a firmament in the midst of the waters, and let it divide the waters from the waters. . . . And God called the firmament Heaven. And the evening and the morning were the second day" (Gen 1:1, 5–8). Sunset, the lilac of the sky, is as ancient as the second day of creation.

But the poem describes the sunset we are witnessing this evening, "The Sun subsiding on his Course" over a nearby hill, which "Bequeathes this final plant." The day is dying, and the expiring sun leaves as a last inheritance "The Flower of Occident," the flower of the west. Unlike the ancient shrub of the opening line, however, this plant cannot be physically grasped, or touched. It is left us for "Contemplation." The stanza breaks here, and the meditation follows in the second stanza.

That meditation opens with an unpacking or explicating of the controlling metaphor of the first stanza: lilac = sunset. Precise botanical terms are used: the *corolla* is the collective term for the petals of a flower that form a ring around the reproductive organs and are surrounded by an outer ring of sepals; the *calyx* is the group of sepals, usually green, around the outside of a flower that protects the flower bud; and the *capsule* is the fruit containing seeds that are released when the flower is mature. Think about a dandelion: its gold petals, green sepals, and mature feathery seeds that are carried away by the wind. Similarly, as a lilac's flowers fade they develop into brown seed pods. In the sunset, the pinks and lavenders of the western sky are the petals, the green earth the calyx, and the glowing evening stars that gradually emerge are the burnished (shimmering) seeds, as the dying sun gives birth to other distant suns.

This explication uses technical scientific terms, which Dickinson knew from her study of botany at Amherst Academy and employed in constructing her herbarium, and she now mockingly terms herself a "Scientist of Faith," who conducts "research" and performs the technical activities of "Synthesis" and "Analysis." Such an approach is limited, however. The research "has but just begun," and the "Flora" (another scientific term) is "unimpeachable," impossible to discredit or challenge, so good that it is beyond reproach. Neither unpacking the metaphor nor scientifically explaining flowers/sunsets capture the full glorious reality, which can only be perceived for oneself. Twenty poems about sunsets do not even begin to approach the beauty of a single living sunset.

Line 17 quotes 1 Cor 2:9, "Eye hath not seen, nor ear heard, neither have entered into the heart of man, the things which God hath prepared for them that love him." The poet takes exception to this verse, suggesting that it "may possibly / Be current with the Blind," but those who are capable of seeing a sunset might have experienced a glimpse of heaven. Indeed, Paul continues in verse 10, "But God hath revealed them unto us by his Spirit." We are able to imagine, to see in images, what God has prepared for us because of the work of the Spirit. "Let not Revelation / By Theses be detained," the poem concludes, referring both to Paul's account of revelation of the Spirit as well as the Book of Revelation, which uses vivid images to describe the heaven that is to come. Theses, argumentative propositions associated with analysis and synthesis, ought not to detain the magnificent revelation of God granted to us through a sunset. If we open our eyes of faith, with the help of the Spirit, we will see God.

Devotion 26

Poem 1280F (1258J)

Who were "the Father and the Son"
We pondered when a child –
And what had they to do with us
And when portentous told

With inference appalling
By Distance fortified
We thought, at least they are no worse
Than they have been described.

Who are "the Father and the Son"
Did we demand Today
"The Father and the Son" himself
Would doubtless specify –

But had they the felicity
When we desired to know,
We better Friends had been, perhaps,
Than time ensue to be –

We start – to learn that we believe
But once – entirely –
Belief, it does not fit so well
When altered frequently –

We blush – that Heaven if we achieve –
Event ineffable –
We shall have shunned until ashamed
To own the Miracle –

Consider: How do you think about God now as opposed to how you thought about God when you were young? Why do you think differently now (if you do)?

Although she originally wrote this poem using the pronoun "I," Dickinson later shifted the voice to speak in a collective "we," suggesting that the experiences and feelings she describes are shared by many people. The poem outlines the differences between our childish views of God "the Father and the Son" and our current views. It's curious that the third member of the Trinity is not mentioned here; all the focus is on the first two members, who are mentioned by name, in quotation marks, three times. But this may echo the way that in the Gospels Jesus repeatedly links understanding his identity with understanding the identity of the Father: "He that hath seen me hath seen the Father. . . . I am in the Father, and the Father in me" (John 14:9, 10).

As children we "pondered," like Mary, not only the identity of the Father and the Son but also the terms of their relationship with us. Someone, unnamed in the poem, "told" us the news, described God to us, and it was not good news. The words *portentous, inference,* and *appalling* all suggest a looming future with dire consequences. (The first version of the poem used "in terror" instead of "portentous.") Yet we are "fortified" by "Distance"; as children, our future encounter with a judging God seems as if it were a long way off. We thus reach a somewhat wry conclusion: "at least they are no worse / Than they have been described."

In the third stanza, we speculate upon what would happen were we to ask the same questions today: who is God the Father and the Son, and how do we stand in relationship to them? It's important to note that we don't actually ask these questions; the conditional sense of "did" and "would" indicate that this is a thought experiment. Far from childish pondering, though, our current inquiries would come in the form of a "demand." And the answer would be markedly different from the earlier

inquiry: it would come directly from God "himself" and would unquestionably, "doubtless," be specific rather than ambiguous.

The poet (and those for whom she speaks) resents the fact that God
did not give these answers much earlier. Had the Father and the Son "the
felicity" to respond back when we first asked and longed to know God,
"We better Friends had been, perhaps." *Felicity* both prompts happiness
and implies appropriateness and is ingeniously associated with *Friends*
through alliteration. The word *better* in line 15 is extremely significant,
because it implies that the speaker has a friendship with God, but their
relationship could be improved. Time has been wasted. Rather than blam-
ing God, however, as the poem appears to do, perhaps we might reflect on
the role of the one who first "told" such grim news to a child and how we
talk to children about the Father and the Son.

"We start"—enacted with a characteristic Dickinsonian dash used
for the first time in this poem in the middle of a line—points in two directions. We are surprised or startled to learn something about belief, but
we also are beginning to learn it for the first time. We now realize that a
complete or entire belief occurs only "once" and that a belief that is "altered frequently" no longer fits as well as the first conviction. Lines 19 and
20, with their implied metaphor of clothing, remind us of "To mend each
tattered Faith," but may incline us to accept the "specious" reading with its
less than enthusiastic endorsement of the effects of changing faith.

"We blush"—with another mid-line dash—indicating our discom-
bobulation and chagrin. The final stanza enacts this confusion in its ambiguous syntax. It seems to be saying that we are embarrassed that we
"shunned" heaven so long, perhaps because of the false idea of God that
we picked up as a child, so embarrassed that we have become "ashamed
/ To own the Miracle." Whether the (collective) speaker of the poem
reaches heaven is unclear; the "if" of line 21 and the description of the
"Event" as "ineffable," or indescribable, obscures whether we have, in fact,
"owned" the Miracle. And yet, we have the poem . . . which Dickinson
sent to Higginson in its revised state.

Devotion 27

Poem 1378F (1311J)

This dirty – little – Heart
Is freely mine –
I won it with a Bun –
A Freckled shrine –

But eligibly fair
To him who sees
The Visage of the Soul
And not the knees.

Consider: How might we observe the appearance of someone's soul? What would allow us to see this immaterial essence?

When she was in her forties, Dickinson saw fewer people, but she continued to interact with the neighborhood children, who often gathered to play in the Dickinson gardens and grounds. When one of these children, MacGregor Jenkins, grew up, he wrote a book about his childhood memories of this unusual woman, who was adored by all the neighborhood children. While he, his sister Sally, Martha Dickinson (Emily's niece, the daughter of Austin and Sue), and Alice Mather played hide-and-seek, the Battle of Bunker Hill (fought with apples), or Pirates, they would often see Emily caring for her potted plants outside the back door of the Homestead. When they were hungry, she would help them raid the kitchen for cookies or doughnuts. In another favorite game, the children pretended to be roaming gypsies, searching for provisions until a signal appeared in Emily's second-floor bedroom window, followed by a basket full of warm gingerbread slowly lowered to the ground.

Dickinson's joyful friendships with such children are celebrated in the opening of this short poem. The "dirty – little – Heart" may describe one of the disheveled children playing pirates in the Dickinson gardens who became devoted to Emily, a fairy godmother in the sky magically bestowing sticky buns and gingerbread. The child "freely" gives her his heart, his affection and admiration. The sing-songy "won it with a Bun" sounds like a nursery rhyme, reinforcing the sense of childish delight and joy. Dickinson thus becomes "A Freckled shrine"—a funny, self-deprecating portrait of the object of childish worship.

The poem takes a more serious tone in the second stanza, signaled by the opening transitional "But." The dirty Heart is now described as "eligibly fair," that is suitably clean, if one knows how to look. That more informed perception comes from examining "The Visage of the Soul / And not the knees." The comical turn in these final two lines is created with an abrupt switch from the grand capitalized language of "Visage" (rather than the simpler "face") to the simple, single-syllable words that conclude with the unexpected image of "knees." The exact rhyme of *sees* and *knees* further emphasizes the childlike tone. From personal experience, I know, just like Dickinson, that a child playing outside all day can have some astonishingly grimy knees, a fact that might have dismayed more fastidious Amherst women.

We're thus reminded of the need to look beyond the external griminess of the lives of people we meet, to recognize the features of their souls. Emily Dickinson tried to look this way upon everyone. It's how God sees, too, as Yahweh reminded Samuel as he surveyed the tall, strong, handsome son of Jesse named Eliab: "Look not on his countenance or on the height of his stature; because I have refused him: for the Lord seeth not as man seeth; for man looketh on the outward appearance, but the Lord looketh on the heart" (1 Sam 16:7).

Devotion 28

Poem 1459F (1433J)

How brittle are the Piers
On which our Faith doth tread –
No Bridge below doth totter so –
Yet none hath such a Crowd.
It is as old as God –
Indeed – 'twas built by him –
He sent his Son to test the Plank –
And he pronounced it firm.

Consider: What do you think the metaphor of the bridge represent?

The bridge that is the controlling metaphor of this poem may have been inspired by the Sunderland Bridge, a privately-owned toll bridge spanning the Connecticut River in which Emily's father was an investor. A Sunderland bridge was a risky enterprise; the high water and ice flows of early-spring thaws destroyed the first nine bridges that were constructed during the nineteenth century. It wasn't until 1938 that a tenth bridge finally was constructed with piers high enough to withstand the elements, a bridge that still stands today. Edward Dickinson's investment in the seventh bridge was destroyed in 1876 when gale-force winds blew the bridge down, and Franklin estimates that this poem was written in 1878.

Nineteenth-century bridge construction was a booming technology, accompanying the widespread development of railroads (in which Edward Dickinson also invested). New and safer techniques were constantly being refined, with scientific stress analysis playing a major role in bridge development. An earlier composition, Poem 978, depicts a strong bridge without piers, but this one opens by describing a particularly fragile bridge that is resting on "brittle" piers—hard, breakable, and lacking durability. The description alludes to the fragility of earthly bridges, such as the recently destroyed Sunderland Bridge, comparing a "Bridge below" with a heavenly or spiritual bridge on which Faith walks, which is even more delicate. While clumsy-footed Faith "treads" heavily, the bridge "totters." But despite the perilous footing, this bridge is crowded, full of believers, and such a surfeit of humanity no doubt also adds to the bridge's instability. Even the rhyme is clunky, confined to the final consonant: trea*d*/crow*d*. Walking by Faith is tentative, potentially dangerous, liable to collapse, yet many people nonetheless continue this journey.

What exactly does the metaphor of the bridge represent? It is the surface on which those who have faith walk, moving from one spot to another, across some kind of chasm. Could it refer to death? Or might it represent the means of grace by which human beings reach God?

The second quatrain tells us more about the bridge: "It is as old as God," that is, eternal, everlasting. "Indeed," line 6 continues, God is the structural engineer, the master builder of the bridge. As a history of bridge building written by the Chief of the National Park Service states, "Since the beginning of time, the goal of bridge builders has been to create as wide a span as possible which is commodious, firm, and occasionally delightful. Spanning greater distances is a distinct measure of engineering prowess."[1] This brittle old bridge built by God spans the greatest possible distance; God's engineering prowess is indeed impressive.

The closing couplet of the poem provides an unexpected turn in the flow of ideas, a sudden confidence that is reinforced by simple sentence structure and clear syntax: "He sent his Son to test the Plank - / And he pronounced it firm." God dispatched his son, Jesus Christ, to try the bridge, and Christ declared that it was safe to cross. The ancient nature of the bridge is reinforced by the additional fact that it is an old-fashioned wooden structure, not the latest nineteenth-century iron and steel engineering wonder. But the word *Plank* also reminds us of the wooden cross on which Christ died.

Because Jesus has gone before us through death and on to resurrection life, we, too, can cross the tottering bridge. While this crowded and

---

1. DeLony, "Scientific Analysis of Bridge Design."

poorly supported bridge may not appear to be the most reliable method of crossing the gap, Jesus' example and proclamation assures us that the bridge is solid. Death is an uncertain experience, yet Christ's death both proves and provides the bridge—the means of grace by which to reach God.

Devotion 29

Poem 1537F (1492J)

"And with what Body do they come"?
Then they *do* come, Rejoice!
What Door – what Hour – Run – run – My Soul!
Illuminate the House!
"Body"! Then real – a Face – and Eyes –
To know that it is them! –
Paul knew the Man that knew the News –
He passed through Bethlehem –

Consider: What is the significance of a bodily resurrection?

The first letter that the apostle Paul wrote to the troubled church at
Corinth reaches a crashing crescendo in the penultimate chapter as Paul
rehearses the evidence for Christ's resurrection and then proclaims the
consequences for humanity: "But now is Christ risen from the dead, and
become the firstfruits of them that slept. For since by man came death,
by man came also the resurrection of the dead. For as in Adam all die,
even so in Christ shall all be made alive" (1 Cor 15:20–22). Given her
perpetual anxiety about the question of life after death, Emily Dickinson
was intrigued with this scriptural account of the resurrection of the dead,
which appeared in one of her favorite chapters of the Bible. And given
her customary contrariness, it is not surprising to find her especially interested in the hypothetical challenge to the idea of the resurrection that
Paul poses in verse 35: "But some man will say, How are the dead raised
up? And with what body do they come?"

Opening Poem 1537 by quoting the second question of verse 35, Dickinson shows no interest in the scientific or mystical explanations implied by the first question as to *how* the dead are raised up. Rather, her attention zeroes in on the fact that "they *do* come"; that, as her italics indicate, those she has known and loved—her mother, father, nephew—will be recognizable at the time of resurrection. The only change Dickinson makes from the original King James text in her quotation is to capitalize *Body*. Further corporeal emphasis occurs with the repeated quotation of this crucial word in line 5, followed by the second of four exclamation points, all of which urge both Dickinson and her readers to "Rejoice!"

The poet's joyful agitation at the idea of the resurrection of the body also emerges in the disjointed questions and exhortations of the third and fourth lines: What door will my loved ones come through? When will they come? Get ready for their arrival by lighting all the lamps in the house! By prompting her (immaterial) "Soul" to (physically) "run" to prepare the "House," the poet affirms a non-dualistic definition of human existence in which body and soul are inextricably connected. The House that requires preparation also evokes Jesus' promise that he is going "to prepare a place for you" in "my father's house" (John 14:2).

The resurrection life depicted in this poem does not consist of romantic disembodied spirits or pantheistic universal souls, but rather concrete bodies with faces and eyes. The poet enthuses, "To know that it is them!" The next line playfully toys with the idea of "knowing" with punning repetition: "Paul *knew* the Man that *knew* the News." That Man is, of course, Jesus Christ, incarnated in a physical body through his birth, but who merely passed through Bethlehem on his way first to the cross and ultimately the resurrection. The "News," then is the good news of the Gospel.

The theologian N. T. Wright has written eloquently about the same scriptural passage that Dickinson ponders in this poem. First-century Jews, he asserts, understood the resurrection not as a state of "disembodied bliss" but rather as "re-embodiment."[1] Wright explains about 1 Cor 15:35–42: "Paul states clearly and emphatically his belief in a body that is to be *changed*, not abandoned. The present physicality in all its transience, its decay and its subjection to weakness, sickness and death, is not to go on and on forever; that is what he means by saying 'flesh and blood

1. Wright, *The Challenge of Jesus*, 134.

cannot inherit the kingdom of God.' For Paul 'flesh and blood' does not mean 'physicality' per se but the corruptible and decaying present state of our physicality."[2] Paul thus answers the question of what kind of body we will have at the resurrection by explaining that our present corruptible physical body will be transformed into a new incorruptible physical body.

Wright notes that the physicality of the resurrection has often been misunderstood or muted by the Christian church, and it is easy to imagine Dickinson's frustration with nineteenth-century sentimental depictions of a heaven full of "Soft – Cherubic Creatures" instead of "freckled Human Nature" (Poem 675). I have always hoped, however, that my freckles will be gone at my resurrection and that I will then possess something resembling my eighteen-year-old body. In Poem 1537 Dickinson rejoices in that kind of physical resurrection. Enclosed in a letter to her cousin Perez Dickinson Cowan upon the death of his young daughter Margaret in 1879, this poem provides powerful comfort in the face of death.

2. Ibid., 143.

Bibliography

Bianchi, Martha Dickinson. *The Life and Letters of Emily Dickinson, by Her Niece.* Boston: Houghton Mifflin, 1924.

DeLony, Eric. "Scientific Analysis of Bridge Design during the 19th Century." In *Context for World Heritage Bridges.* Paris: ICOMOS and TICCIH, 1996. http://www.icomos. org/studies/bridges.htm#11.

Dickinson, Emily. *The Letters of Emily Dickinson.* Edited by Thomas H. Johnson. Cambridge, MA: Belknap, 1960.

———. *The Poems of Emily Dickinson.* Edited by Thomas H. Johnson. Cambridge, MA: Belknap, 1983.

———. *The Poems of Emily Dickinson: Reading Edition.* Edited by Ralph W. Franklin. Cambridge: MA: Belknap, 1999.

———. *The Poems of Emily Dickinson: Variorum Edition.* Edited by Ralph W. Franklin. Cambridge: MA: Belknap, 1998.

Doriani, Beth Maclay. *Emily Dickinson, Daughter of Prophecy.* Amherst: University of Massachusetts Press, 1996.

Gallagher, Susan V., and Roger Lundin. *Literature through the Eyes of Faith.* San Francisco: Harper & Row, 1989.

Habegger, Alfred. *My Wars Are Laid Away in Books: The Life of Emily Dickinson.* New York: Modern Library, 2001.

Jenkins, MacGregor. *Emily Dickinson: Friend and Neighbor.* Boston: Little, Brown, 1939.

Noll, Mark A. *America's God: From Jonathan Edwards to Abraham Lincoln.* Oxford: Oxford University Press, 2002.

Sewall, Richard B. *The Life of Emily Dickinson.* 2 vols. New York: Farrar, Straus, and Giroux, 1974.

———. *The Lyman Letters: New Light on Emily Dickinson and Her Family.* Amherst: University of Massachusetts Press, 1965.

Walker, Jeanne Murray. "A Comment on the State of the Art: Poetry in 2004." *Christianity and Literature* 54 (2004) 93–110.

Wright, N.T. *The Challenge of Jesus: Rediscovering Who Jesus Was and Is.* Downers Grove, IL: InterVarsity, 1999.